Illuminate Publishing

Blood Brothers
Play Guide

for AQA GCSE Drama

Annie Fox

Published in 2019 by Illuminate Publishing Ltd, P.O. Box 1160, Cheltenham, Gloucestershire GL50 9RW

Orders: Please visit www.illuminatepublishing.com or email sales@illuminatepublishing.com

© 2019 Annie Fox

The moral rights of the author have been asserted.

All rights reserved. No part of this book may be reprinted, reproduced or utilised in any form or by any electronic, mechanical, or other means, now known or hereafter invented, including photocopying and recording, or in any information storage and retrieval system, without permission in writing from the publishers.

British Library Cataloguing in Publication Data

A catalogue record for this book is available from the British Library.

ISBN 978 1 911208 70 9

Printed in Wales by Cambrian Printers Ltd

06.21

The publisher's policy is to use papers that are natural, renewable and recyclable products made from wood grown in sustainable forests. The logging and manufacturing processes are expected to conform to the environmental regulations of the country of origin.

Every effort has been made to contact copyright holders of material reproduced in this book. Great care has been taken by the author and publishers to ensure that either formal permission has been granted for the use of copyright material reproduced, or that copyright material has been used under fair-dealing guidelines in the UK – specifically that it has been used sparingly, for the purpose of criticism and review, and has been properly acknowledged. If notified, the publishers will be pleased to rectify any errors or omissions at the earliest opportunity.

Editor: Roanne Charles, abc Editorial
Design and layout: Neil Sutton, Cambridge Design Consultants
Cover design: Neil Sutton, Cambridge Design Consultants. Cover photograph: WENN Ltd / Alamy Stock Photo

Text acknowledgements

Extracts in this book are taken from *Blood Brothers* by Willy Russell, Methuen Modern Classics; p32 extracts from 'Willy Russell: "I want to talk about things that matter"' by Angela Levin © Telegraph Media Group Limited 2012; p86 extract from 'Summer and Smoke, Almeida Theatre, London, review' by Holly Williams © *Independent*, 8 March 2018, extract from 'Review: Summer and Smoke' by Daisy Bowie-Sell reproduced with the kind permission of WhatsOnStage.com.

Picture acknowledgements

pp4 bottom and 51 top right bloodbrothersthemusical.com; pp6–8, 13 left, 14 right, 15 top, 16 and 17 top, 18 top, 28 top, 20–21, 33 top, 38 bottom, 39, 43, 57 (stage), 72–74, 90, 92, 102, 116, 121 and 136 emc design; pp11, 28–29, 34, 44, 46, 48–50, 57 (scaffold), 58–59 and 131 Neil Sutton; p12 1 and 2, 84, 85 left, 99, 100 top and bottom, 107, 108, 112 and 116 © Paul Fox; p12 3 Joan Marcus; p13 right Tony Bartholemew; pp14 left and 18 Granger Historical Picture Archive / Alamy Stock Photo; p15 bottom Sheffield Theatres; p16 bottom King's Cross Theatre; p17 bottom Richard Lakos; p18 bottom Robin Roemer; pp22 and 51 left Keith Pattison; p30 bottom Rod Varley / Alamy Stock Photo; pp31, 45 and 47 Trinity Mirror / Mirrorpix / Alamy Stock Photo; p32 top jeremy sutton-hibbert / Alamy Stock Photo; pp32 bottom and 94–95 Manuel Harlan; p33 left Collection Christophel / Alamy Stock Photo, right ClassicStock / Alamy Stock Photo; p35 Barry Lewis / Alamy Stock Photo; p36 left Homer Sykes / Alamy Stock Photo, right INTERFOTO / Alamy Stock Photo; p38 top Allan Cash Picture Library / Alamy Stock Photo; p51 bottom right Preston Theatres; p60 WENN Ltd / Alamy Stock Photo; p64 top Pictorial Press Ltd / Alamy Stock Photo; pp82 and 128 Alastair Muir; pp85 right and 87 Marc Brenner; p85 bottom Helen Murray; p88 Geraint Lewis / Alamy Stock Photo; p91 Sueddeutsche Zeitung Photo / Alamy Stock Photo; p96 Broadway.com; p100 right © Steve Tanner / Kneehigh; p109 Johan Persson; p117 Bettina Strenske / Alamy Stock Photo.

All other images **Shutterstock**: p4 top Iakov Filimonov; pp24–25 and 49 S-F; p30 top Alexander Lukatskiy; p40 tomertu; p64 bottom Aleshyn_Andrei; p97 top left Pavel L Photo and Video / Shutterstock.com, top right criben/Shutterstock.com, bottom left evgenii mitroshin, bottom right Oleinik Iuliia / Shutterstock.com; p111 Tito Wong, p114 Oleinik Iuliia / Shutterstock.com; p115 Feng Yu; pp118–119 agusyonok; p124 Monkey Business Images; p132 Nukul Chanada

CONTENTS

INTRODUCTION

This Play Guide is designed to help you to succeed in all aspects of Component 1 of AQA GCSE Drama, focusing on Willy Russell's *Blood Brothers* as your set text for Section B. You might use the book alongside the work you are doing in your lessons at school or to help you with your independent revision. Throughout this book, there are creative tasks, sample exam questions and suggested answers, as well as helpful opportunities to check and stretch your learning.

What is Component 1?

Component 1 of GCSE Drama is 'Understanding drama'. The exam is a written one that consists of three sections, with a total of 80 marks:

▶ Section A: Theatre roles and terminology (4 marks)
▶ Section B: Study of a set text (44 marks)
▶ Section C: Live theatre production (32 marks).

It accounts for 40 per cent of the GCSE Drama assessment. (The remainder being the practical components 'Devising drama' and 'Texts in practice'.)

How are you assessed?

The exam assesses your:

▶ knowledge and understanding of drama and theatre
▶ study of one set play (from a choice of six)
▶ analysis and evaluation of the work of live theatre makers.

Section A: Theatre roles and terminology

This part of the exam consists of multiple-choice questions on topics such as:

▶ the roles and responsibilities of theatre makers
▶ the features of different staging configurations
▶ the correct terms for different positions on stage.

Section B: Study of a set text

This section contains questions about the particular set text you have studied. You will be presented with an extract from the set play. The first three questions are compulsory for all students, then you will need to choose to answer either the fourth or fifth question. Topics covered typically include:

▶ using design to convey the context of the play
▶ vocal and physical performance skills
▶ use of stage space and interaction between characters
▶ one question with a choice of performance or design specialism.

You will need to write paragraphs in response to these questions, although you might also, if you choose, include sketches to support your design ideas. You should aim for well-organised responses that use specialist vocabulary appropriately.

Section C: Live theatre production

Section C consists of three questions. You will choose one to answer in reference to a live drama production. The questions will ask you to describe, analyse and evaluate either a performance aspect or design aspect of the production you have seen.

How to use this book

This book is designed to cover all aspects of Component 1 for those studying *Blood Brothers* as their set text. There are chapters devoted to each section of the written exam, as well as a chapter on improving your writing and exam skills. There is also a glossary that provides a useful reference and will help you to improve your use of technical terms. There are many examples of exam-style questions for you to practise essay writing and other responses within time limits.

You may choose to work through the book in any order that you like, but, to make full use of the guidance and ideas offered for the whole exam, make sure you cover all sections. There is a crossover in the different skills developed in the various sections, so that you might find, for example, the technical vocabulary explained in Section C helpful to your writing in Section B. Understanding the different staging configurations and positions explained in Section A might also be helpful when writing about design or performances in Sections B and C.

Some special features to help you get the most from the book include:

 Tips: Guidance for the exam and how to avoid common errors.

Tasks: Practical activities to improve your learning. These include, for example, experimenting with acting skills on particular extracts, sketching costume and set designs or evaluating sample answers.

Key terms: Definitions of drama vocabulary to help you understand how drama works and to express your ideas fluently and appropriately. These are also gathered in a glossary at the back of the book as a reference resource.

 Test yourself: A set of quick questions that revise key ideas and terms covered in the preceding guidance pages.

Learning checklist: A review at the end of a topic in which you can assess your learning and decide which areas require more revision.

What the specification says: Notes on the assessment objectives and the demands of the specification.

Practice questions: A range of exam-style questions for you to attempt, ideally under exam-type conditions.

Sample answers: Candidate-style responses to exam-type questions, annotated to show where marks might be gained or lost.

 Look here: Suggestions on where you can find more information about a given topic elsewhere in this book.

 Check it out: References to the *AQA GCSE Drama* coursebook, for additional information and details.

 Pages that are available to download and print as worksheets from www.illuminatepublishing.com/drama.

 TIP

Be aware of how many marks different questions are worth and organise your revision appropriately. A good approach is to spend the most time preparing for the questions worth the most marks.

 TIP

If you need more assistance with the course, including Components 2 and 3, try the accompanying *AQA GCSE Drama* book, which covers all the set texts and all the components of the AQA GCSE Drama course.

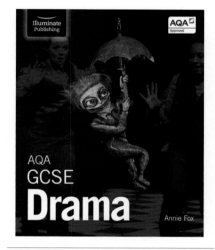

 TEST YOURSELF 1

1 In which section of the exam will you write about a live theatre production you have seen?

2 How many questions in total are you required to answer in Section B?

3 Which section of the exam (A, B or C) is worth the most marks?

4 The written exam is worth what percentage of your Drama GCSE?

5 Which section of the exam consists of multiple-choice questions?

6 Besides the 'key terms' notes, where in this book will you find definitions of drama vocabulary?

THEATRE ROLES AND TERMINOLOGY

What the specification says...

The specification requires you to have knowledge of how theatre works in a practical way. In order to express yourself accurately when writing about drama, you need to understand:

▸ the different ways plays could be staged

▸ what the advantages and challenges of different theatre configurations are

▸ who is responsible for different elements of a production.

Students must develop knowledge and understanding of:

▸ Drama and theatre terminology and how to use it appropriately:
  – stage positioning
  – staging configurations.

Students should have a general understanding of the implications of the above stage configurations on the use of the performance space.

▸ The roles and responsibilities of theatre makers in contemporary professional practice.
  Knowledge and understanding should cover:
  – the activities each might undertake on a day-to-day basis
  – the aspects of the rehearsal/performance process each is accountable for (their contribution to the whole production being a success).

You will be assessed by:

▸ multiple-choice questions.

The names and roles of theatre makers

Many different people are involved with creating a successful production of a theatrical performance. Key people whose roles you should understand include:

PLAYWRIGHT

Writes the script of the play, including dialogue and stage directions.

PERFORMER

Appears in a production, for example, acting, dancing or singing.

Creates a performance or assumes a role on stage in front of an audience.

DIRECTOR

Oversees and manages the creative aspects of the production.

Develops a 'concept' or central unifying idea for the production.

Liaises with designers, rehearses the performers and ensures that all elements of the production are ready.

Blocks the movements of the actors and gives 'notes' to improve performances.

THEATRE MANAGER

In charge of the theatre building, including overseeing the front of house and box office staff who sell tickets and liaise with the public.

UNDERSTUDY

Learns a part, including lines and movements, so they are able to take over a role for someone, if needed, when there is a planned or unexpected absence.

STAGE MANAGER

Runs the backstage elements of the play, and supervises the backstage crew.

Organises the rehearsal schedule and keeps lists of props and other technical needs.

Creates a prompt book and calls the cues for the performance.

TECHNICIAN

Operates the technical equipment, such as lighting and sound boards, during the performance.

SOUND DESIGNER

Designs the sound required for the performance, which might include music and sound effects.

Creates a sound plot.

Takes appropriate action if amplification, such as the use of microphones, is needed.

LIGHTING DESIGNER

Designs the lighting states and effects that will be used in a performance.

Understands the technical capabilities of the theatre and creates a lighting plot accordingly.

COSTUME DESIGNER

Designs what the actors wear on stage.

Provides sketches and other design materials.

Ensures that costumes are appropriate for the play and fit the performers.

SET DESIGNER

Designs the set and, if needed, the set dressings (objects placed on the stage).

Provides sketches and other design materials, before overseeing the creation of the set.

PUPPET DESIGNER

Designs the puppets for a production, as needed, taking into account the style of the puppets and how they will be operated.

KEY TERMS

Block: Set the movements made by the actors.

Front of house: Ushers and other members of theatre staff who deal with the audience, as opposed to those who work backstage.

Prompt book: A copy of the production script of the play, which includes detailed information about the play's blocking, props and other technical elements.

Call the cues: Announce instructions, for example, telling technicians when lighting or sound changes should occur.

Sound plot: A list of the sound effects or music needed and any sound equipment that will be used. This is usually organised scene-by-scene and might contain information such as cues and volume.

Amplification: How sounds are made louder, usually through the use of microphones or other sound-boosting equipment.

Lighting states: The settings and positions of lighting to create certain lighting conditions, such as a bright afternoon or a moonlit scene.

Lighting plot: A guide to the lighting of a production, including the location and types of various lighting instruments and a scene-by-scene list of lighting requirements.

Who is responsible for what and when in theatre making?

BEFORE REHEARSALS

- ▸ Stage manager and technicians are hired.

- ▸ Once cast, performers begin to prepare their roles.

- ▸ The director decides on the **concept** of the production and casts the performers.

- ▸ The playwright produces a script.

- ▸ Designers produce initial designs – for sets, costumes and lighting, for example – and begin any pre-production work.

- ▸ The theatre manager agrees the use of theatre and prepares it for the production.

DURING REHEARSALS

- ▸ The theatre manager ensures the theatre will be ready and relevant staff are hired.

- ▸ Designers realise their designs, including costume fittings, set construction and lighting plots.

- ▸ Understudies learn the role or roles they are **covering**.

- ▸ Performers rehearse their roles, learn lines and blocking.

- ▸ The stage manager notes the blocking, creates rehearsal lists and prepares the prompt book.

- ▸ The director leads rehearsals with performers.

DURING PERFORMANCES

- ▸ The stage manager runs the show, using the prompt book, and calls the cues.

- ▸ Technicians operate technical equipment, such as sound and lighting boards.

- ▸ The theatre manager ensures front of house is run smoothly.

- ▸ Understudies are prepared to go on stage if a performer is unable to.

- ▸ Performers present their roles before an audience.

TIP

Some productions will vary from the typical roles and responsibilities listed on these two pages. For example, some shows don't start with a script, but are devised as they go along. In some productions, members of the cast also take on backstage roles or the direction of the play. The exam, however, will be based on the typical division of responsibilities as explained here.

KEY TERMS

Concept: A unifying idea about the production, such as how it will be interpreted and performed.

Covering (a role): Learning the words and movements for a part that you do not usually perform.

CHECK IT OUT

See page 18 of *AQA GCSE Drama* for three short interviews in which theatre makers discuss their roles.

TEST YOURSELF A1

Look at the descriptions below of various theatre makers describing their roles and responsibilities. Match each description to the correct theatre maker.

COSTUME DESIGNER   UNDERSTUDY   TECHNICIAN   STAGE MANAGER

PLAYWRIGHT   THEATRE MANAGER   DIRECTOR   PUPPET DESIGNER

LIGHTING DESIGNER   SOUND DESIGNER   PERFORMER   SET DESIGNER

What the specification says...

Knowledge and understanding should cover:

- The activities each (theatre maker) might undertake on a day-to-day basis
- The aspects of the rehearsal/performance process each is accountable for.

KEY TERMS

Collaborative: A process where people work together rather than individually.

Backdrop: A large painted cloth that serves as scenery, often at the back of the stage.

Projections: A technique where moving or still images are projected to form a theatrical backdrop.

Model box: A three-dimensional scale-model of the set that shows how the real set will look and work.

Lighting rig: The structure that holds the lighting equipment in the theatre (usually in the roof).

Backpack puppets: Large puppets attached to the puppeteer by a backpack-like device.

During the performance, I rely both on a cue sheet and the stage manager calling cues to ensure that I change the lighting at exactly the right moment.

My job is one of the most important. I am responsible for making sure that all of the backstage elements run smoothly, including issuing the calls to the actors; being prepared to prompt if someone forgets a line and calling technical cues.

My primary tools are dialogue and stage directions. I might write several drafts of the script before I am happy with it. Some scripts even change during the rehearsal process.

When I read a script, I note all the opportunities for sound, including music for transitions or sound effects. I think about how sound can affect the atmosphere of the play.

For some shows, particularly if outfits are complex and have to be specially made, I arrange fittings with the actors well before rehearsals. For other shows, I wait until rehearsals and the process is more **collaborative**.

Once the production is scheduled, I make sure that the building is ready to receive the show, including having ushers and box office staff on hand for performances.

My design might be restricted by the technical capabilities of a theatre. If there is only a small **lighting rig**, I might have to limit some of the effects I want. I might be able to come up with solutions such as hand-held lights.

I have to think about the size of the stage and where entrances and exits will occur, as well as any levels or ramps that might be needed. I decide if I want to use **backdrops** or **projections** in my design as well as how scene changes might occur. I then prepare sketches and a **model box**.

When I first read the script, I think about what the play's message is. I develop a concept for the play which will influence how I cast it and when and where I will set it.

I was delighted when I was cast. During rehearsals, the director guided my interpretation of the part, including the blocking of my movements.

I am prepared to assume the role I have been learning if the usual actor is unable to perform. This can be quite nerve-wracking as I won't have had as much time to rehearse as the usual actor.

Some productions demand a lot from my skills. If we are working in a large outdoor space, I design and create large **backpack puppets** that can be seen well at a distance.

What the specification says...

Knowledge and understanding should cover:

- Drama and theatre terminology and how to use it appropriately, including stage positioning:
  - ▸ Upstage (left, right, centre)
  - ▸ Downstage (left, right, centre)
  - ▸ Centre stage.

Stage positioning

In order to note movements in a script or to express locations quickly, theatre makers use subject-specific terminology to describe places on the stage.

The diagram below shows the stage positions of a typical rectangular **end on staging configuration**.

 TIP

To understand if you need to refer to 'right' or 'left,' imagine you are an actor standing on the centre of the stage, facing the audience. Stage right is to your right and stage left is to your left. The left and right refer to the actor's left and right, not the audience's.

KEY TERMS

End on: A staging configuration in which the audience sits along one end of the stage (the front), directly facing it.

Staging configuration: The type of stage and audience arrangement.

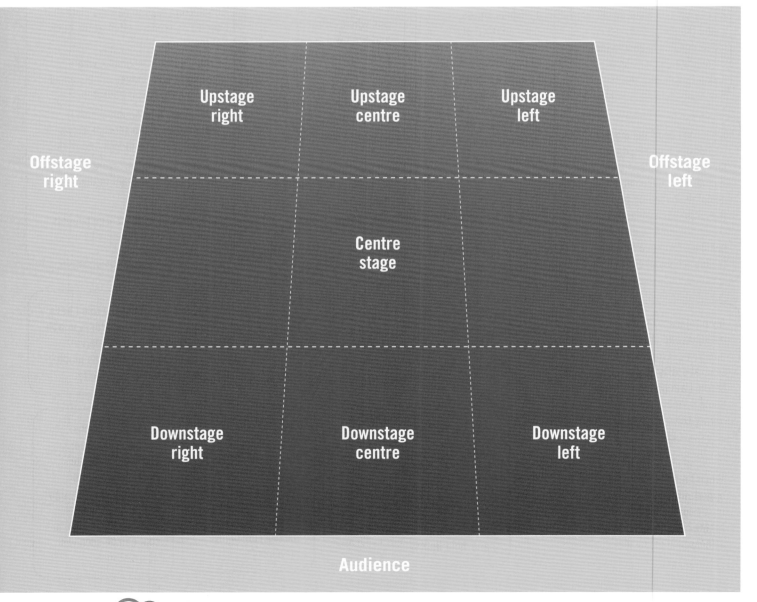

www.illuminatepublishing.com/drama

TASK A1

1 Imagine you are a set designer and the director has asked you to put the following items on stage:

   A A wide doorway, upstage centre

   B A pair of chairs and a table, centre stage

   C A small rug, downstage right

   D A window, upstage left

   E A kitchen sink, stage right.

Use the diagram on the previous page to note where you would put them.

TIP

When describing where characters are in relation to each other, you can use the same stage-positioning terminology. For example, if you have one character standing behind another and they are both facing downstage, you could say that the character behind is standing *upstage* of the other one. If you want a character to move from upstage right to downstage left, you could write that they *cross downstage left*.

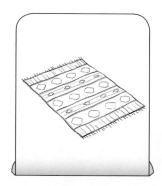

2 Now imagine you are an actor and you have been asked to do the following blocking. Note where on the stage you will be each time.

   A Enter through the wide doorway.

   B Make yourself a cup of tea.

   C Sit down on a chair.

   D Look dreamily out of the window.

   E Stand as close and centrally to the audience as you can.

   F Move as far away from the small rug as you can.

3 Copy a new version of the stage space and decide where you would put entrances or the set needed for the final scene of *Blood Brothers* (page 107), when the Policeman tells everyone not to move. Mark on the diagram where the characters are positioned and annotate it with stage directions. For example, if you have put the Narrator downstage to one side, you might write: *Narrator: downstage left* (or *DSL*).

What the specification says...

Understand drama and theatre terminology and how to use it appropriately:

■ Staging configuration:
  ▸ Theatre in the round
  ▸ Proscenium arch
  ▸ Thrust stage
  ▸ Traverse
  ▸ End on staging
  ▸ Promenade.

Staging configuration

When deciding which staging configuration is best suited to a particular production, some considerations might be:

▸ Whether there is space to store large pieces of scenery to the side of the stage (wings) or above the stage

▸ How scene/set changes will be accomplished

▸ Whether you need curtains to hide scene changes or to create particular effects

▸ How close you want the audience to be to the action

▸ How formal a setting you want

▸ Where entrances and exits will take place

▸ Whether there is any audience interaction

▸ The style and size of your set and its desired effect

▸ Whether it matters if the audience can see one another

▸ Whether you want the audience to move with the action

▸ How important it is for all audience members to see the play from the same perspective

▸ The types of performance the actors will be giving.

 TEST YOURSELF A2

Before you read on for details about staging, try to identify the type of stage configuration in each image below. How can you tell?

1

2

TIP

As you learn about the various staging configurations, think about the advantages and disadvantages of each, as well as the different types of performance that they might suit.

3

Theatre in the round

Theatre in the round is a staging configuration where the audience is seated around all sides of the centrally placed stage.

Theatre in the round ▼

Advantages:

▸ It often suits productions where the audience should be close to the action.

▸ It can encourage **audience interaction** and/or a sense of intimacy.

▸ Entrances and exits are usually made through the audience, which can be exciting.

▸ The audience might feel more involved with the action as there is no obvious '**fourth wall**'.

Challenges:

▸ Blocking must be done carefully, so that certain sections of the audience don't miss key moments of action or dialogue, or facial expressions.

▸ Tall **flats**, backdrops or stage furniture cannot be used, as they will restrict **sightlines**.

▸ The audience can see each other, which can be distracting.

▸ It can be difficult to create a single '**stage picture**' which is sufficiently effective for the whole audience.

▸ It is difficult to put a curtain around the stage, so scene changes might have to occur within the view of the audience.

Task A2

The Stephen Joseph Theatre in Scarborough is a well-known example of a theatre in the round. Look at this photograph from its production of *Confusions* by Alan Ayckbourn. What are the challenges for the set designer and actors of using this configuration?

Stephen Joseph Theatre, Scarborough ▼

KEY TERMS

Audience interaction: Directly involving members of the audience in the play, for example, by bringing them onstage, going into the audience to speak with them, asking for a response from onstage, or passing them props to hold.

Fourth wall: An imaginary wall that separates the actors from the audience, giving the impression that the world of the actors is entirely distinct from that of the audience.

Flats: Pieces of scenery mounted on frames, for example, representing walls.

Sightlines: The view the audience has of the stage and/or dramatic action. If a sightline is blocked or restricted, for example by a poorly placed piece of furniture, it means that some audience members cannot see part of the stage.

Stage picture: A term for a well-arranged visual stage image which conveys a certain impression to the audience. This is also called a 'tableau'.

Proscenium arch stage

A proscenium arch theatre is one of the most common forms of theatre, especially for larger, more formal theatres and opera houses. The proscenium refers to the frame around the stage, which emphasises that the whole audience is seeing the same stage picture. The area in front of the arch is called an **apron**. This is the stage area nearest the audience in front of the curtain.

A proscenium arch stage ▲

Advantages:

▸ The proscenium frame emphasises the stage pictures.

▸ Backdrops and large scenery can be used without interfering with sightlines.

▸ There might be **fly space** and **wing spaces** for storing scenery.

▸ The frame around the stage adds to the effect of the fourth wall, giving the impression of a self-contained world.

▸ When the curtains are down, for example for set changes, scenes might be played in front of the curtain on the stage's apron.

Challenges:

▸ Some audience members might feel distant from the stage.

▸ The auditorium might feel very formal and rigid.

▸ The proscenium frame might seem too old-fashioned to some.

▸ Audience interaction might be more difficult.

Task A3

A famous example of a proscenium arch is in the Royal Opera House in London. Imagine you have been asked to stage the opening of *Blood Brothers* in this configuration. Write a paragraph describing how you would use this staging. Include use of:

● wings/fly space
● curtains
● apron space
● entrances and exits.

The proscenium arch of the Royal Opera House, Covent Garden ▼

KEY TERMS

Apron: The front area of the stage, nearest the audience, which projects in front of the curtain.

Fly space: The area above the stage where scenery might be stored and lowered to the stage.

Wing space: An area to the side of the stage. This is the space where actors, unseen by the audience, wait to enter and where props and set pieces can be stored.

Thrust stage

A thrust stage juts into the auditorium, with the audience arranged on three sides. This is one of the oldest types of theatre stage. Ancient Greek amphitheatres (where the audience was seated in a semicircle around almost half the curved stage) and the theatres in Shakespeare's day (where the audience in the pit stood around three sides of the stage) are both types of thrust stages. In the mid-20th century, they became an increasingly popular staging configuration again, and are used in theatres such as the Crucible Theatre in Sheffield, built in 1971.

A thrust stage ▲

The Crucible Theatre, Sheffield ▼

Task A4

Imagine you have been asked to stage the school scene from *Blood Brothers* (pages 66–67) on a thrust stage. Draw an outline of where you would place the scenery and actors. Remember to consider audience sightlines and the effects you wish to create.

Advantages:

▶ It combines some of the benefits of both proscenium and theatre-in-the-round stages.

▶ As there is no audience on the upstage side of the stage, backdrops, flats, projections and large scenery can be used.

▶ Many members of the audience might feel closer to the performance as there are three first rows – one on each of the stage's three sides – and they are often close to the edge of the stage.

▶ This is often perceived as an exciting space which encourages a connection between the performers and the audience.

Challenges:

▶ Sightlines for those on the extreme sides might be restricted or obstructed.

▶ The audience on the right and left sides of the auditorium have each other in their view.

▶ **Box sets** – where three sides of a room are constructed – cannot be used as they would restrict views for much of the audience.

▶ Not all of the audience members see the stage from the same angle, so stage pictures might be more difficult to create.

KEY TERM

Box set: A set with three complete walls, often used in naturalistic set designs, for example to create a believable room.

Traverse stage

A traverse stage has a long central acting area. The audience is seated on either side of this playing area, facing each other. Although it is relatively rare for a traverse stage to be the permanent staging configuration for a theatre, some flexible theatres rearrange their auditoriums to create this configuration.

Task A5

Make a list of locations which you believe would particularly suit a traverse staging configuration.

A traverse stage

Advantages:

▸ Many audience members will feel very close to the action, as there are two long front rows.

▸ The audience can see the reactions of the other people facing them. This might increase a feeling of involvement and interaction.

▸ It can be used to recreate certain settings with great effect, such as a catwalk, a pavement, a conveyor belt or a railway platform.

▸ The extreme ends of the stage can be used to create additional acting areas.

Challenges:

▸ Large pieces of scenery, stage furniture or backdrops can block sightlines.

▸ The long, thin nature of the acting area can make some blocking tricky.

▸ Actors must be aware of making themselves visible and audible to both sides of the audience.

▸ Lighting needs to be arranged carefully to avoid lights shining into the audience's eyes or spilling onto them.

▸ Some audience members might find being able to see each other distracting and unsettling.

The Railway Children at King's Cross Theatre

End on staging

With end on staging, the audience is seated along one end of the stage, directly facing it. This is similar to a proscenium arch stage, but without the large proscenium frame.

End on staging ▲

Four Play at Theatre 503 ▼

Advantages:

▸ The audience members all have a similar view.

▸ Stage pictures are easy to create.

▸ Large backdrops, projections and box sets can be used.

Challenges:

▸ Audience members at the back might feel distant from the action.

▸ It doesn't have the decorative frame of a proscenium arch theatre and possibly will not have the curtains, which give flexibility in some productions.

▸ The stage might not have the wing and fly spaces associated with large proscenium arch theatres.

KEY TERM

Immersive: A type of theatre where the audience are in the middle of the action of the performance, without the sense of separation usually associated with going to the theatre. They might be required to wear masks, costumes or to follow certain characters.

Promenade

Promenade theatre is a performance setting where there is no formal, separate stage. Instead, the audience members stand or follow the actors through the performance. This might occur in a conventional theatre space, but often promenade productions take place in larger, unconventional spaces such as parks, warehouses or office spaces. Theatre companies such as Punchdrunk and dreamthinkspeak are famous for their innovative and **immersive** promenade productions.

Promenade theatre in a town square ▲

Punchdrunk's Sleep No More, *New York – the audience members are wearing masks.* ▼

Advantages:

▶ There can be exciting design opportunities in converting an unusual space into a performance area.

▶ This is an interactive and exciting type of theatre, where the audience can feel very involved.

▶ This type of staging is likely to enable experimental and new types of theatre.

Challenges:

▶ The audience might find moving around the space difficult or get tired of standing.

▶ Actors or stage crew need to be skilled at moving the audience around and controlling their focus.

▶ There can be health and safety risks.

 TEST YOURSELF A3

Read the descriptions of different staging configurations below and decide which is being described:

THEATRE IN THE ROUND   PROMENADE   TRAVERSE

THRUST   PROSCENIUM ARCH   END ON

Task A6

Now go back to Test yourself A2 on page 12 and check your answers.

A The audience was seated around three sides of the stage. On the upstage wall was a cloth backdrop which looked like a tapestry map of England. Downstage, cushions had been placed to form a seating area.

B All the seats directly faced the stage. The stage itself was a large, rectangular area with wings at either side.

C The audience was seated along two sides of a long narrow acting area. At either end of the performance space was a slightly wider area with two small platforms. As we were facing the other half of the audience, we were very aware of other people's reactions.

D At the centre of the circular stage was a low water fountain and, on the edges of the stage, were several low stools and benches. The actors entered through the audience and regularly moved positions to avoid having their backs to any section of the audience for long periods.

E The audience members were guided into a warehouse. One floor had been converted into a Wild West saloon. The audience stood in groups and watched the actors perform a song before being led to another area.

F When we entered the auditorium, we saw red velvet curtains hanging from a large decorative arch. The curtains were raised to reveal a box set that seemed to take up the entire stage.

Practice questions for Component 1, Section A

You will answer a number of multiple-choice questions in your exam.

Part 1

1 In professional theatre, who is responsible for calling the cues during a show?

    A The theatre manager.

    B The stage manager.

    C The director.

2 When performing in a theatre in the round, which of the following is true?

    A The audience is encouraged to stand and walk around.

    B The audience is arranged on all sides of the playing space.

    C It is easy to use large pieces of scenery or backdrops.

3 What type of stage is shown in this diagram?

    A A thrust stage.

    B A traverse stage.

    C A proscenium arch.

4 With reference to the stage in question 3, in what position is the table?

    A Downstage left.

    B Downstage right.

    C Upstage left.

Part 2

1 In professional theatre, who is responsible for running the theatre building, including making sure it is safe for audience and performers, and ready for the production?

    A The technician.

    B The stage manager.

    C The theatre manager.

2 Which of the following configurations is best suited for a play where you want the actors to enter and exit through the audience and for the audience to be sitting all around the stage space?

    A Theatre in the round.

    B Proscenium arch.

    C End on.

3 What type of stage is shown here?

    A Promenade theatre.

    B Thrust theatre.

    C Proscenium arch theatre.

4 With reference to the stage in question 3, what stage position is the microphone in?

    A Downstage left.

    B Centre stage.

    C Upstage centre.

LEARNING CHECKLIST: SECTION A

Tick each aspect of theatre roles and terminology if you are confident of your knowledge.

If you are unsure of anything, go back and revise.

Do you know...?

- Director
- Performers
- **THE ROLES AND RESPONSIBILITIES OF THEATRE MAKERS**
- Designers
- Technicians
- Stage manager

- Before rehearsals
- **THEATRE MAKERS' BASIC RESPONSIBILITIES**
- During rehearsals
- During performances

- The difference between upstage and downstage
- **THE NAMES FOR THE DIFFERENT POSITIONS ON STAGE**
- Where stage right and stage left are
- How to locate where an object or character is on the stage when told what its position is (such as downstage left or centre stage)

- Theatre in the round
- Thrust
- Promenade
- **HOW TO DESCRIBE THE DIFFERENT STAGING CONFIGURATIONS**
- Proscenium arch
- Traverse
- Advantages and challenges
- End on
- How to identify the different staging configurations from a sketch or photograph

SECTION B

STUDY OF A SET PLAY: BLOOD BROTHERS

What the specification says...

Students are expected to know and understand:

▶ the characteristics and context of the whole play they have studied.

One extract from each set play is printed in the question paper.

Students answer questions relating to that extract, referring to the whole play as appropriate to the demands of the question.

Assessment focus:

AO3: Demonstrate knowledge and understanding of how drama and theatre are developed and performed.

Sean Jones as Mickey and Simon Willmont as Eddie in *Blood Brothers*

For Component 1, Section B, you will study one of six set plays. One of these set plays is *Blood Brothers* by Willy Russell, which is covered in detail in this chapter. All page numbers given refer to the Methuen Drama Modern Classics edition of the play (ISBN 978-0-413-76770-7).

The features of drama

In Section B, you will have the opportunity to share your understanding of *Blood Brothers* and your ideas about how it could be performed and designed.

Writing about drama is different from writing an English Literature essay. In Drama, you are expected to demonstrate a **practical** understanding of how acting and design choices can create a particular **interpretation** of a text and how those choices will have an impact on the audience.

Characteristics of a play

▶ **Genre**   ▶ **Style**
▶ **Plot**   ▶ **Characters**.

Context

▶ The time period in which the play is set
▶ The location of the play
▶ The political or social concerns expressed in the play
▶ The fashions of the time
▶ The music, entertainments and other cultural factors of the time
▶ The backgrounds of the characters.

Examples of practical understanding

▶ How a play could be acted, including physical and vocal skills
▶ How it could be staged, including staging configuration and placement of characters on stage
▶ How it could be designed, including costumes, set, props, lighting and sound.

KEY TERMS

Practical: Something that can actually be physically done, rather than simply an idea.

Interpretation: Bringing out a particular meaning by making specific choices. In this case, how a play could be performed or designed in order to get across a particular meaning. There might be many different interpretations possible.

Genre: A category or type of music, art or literature, usually with its own typical conventions.

Plot: The sequence of main events of a play, film or novel.

Style: The way in which something is created or performed.

Characters: The people involved in the action of a play, film or novel.

 **TEST YOURSELF B1**

Match the theatrical term with its correct application to *Blood Brothers*.

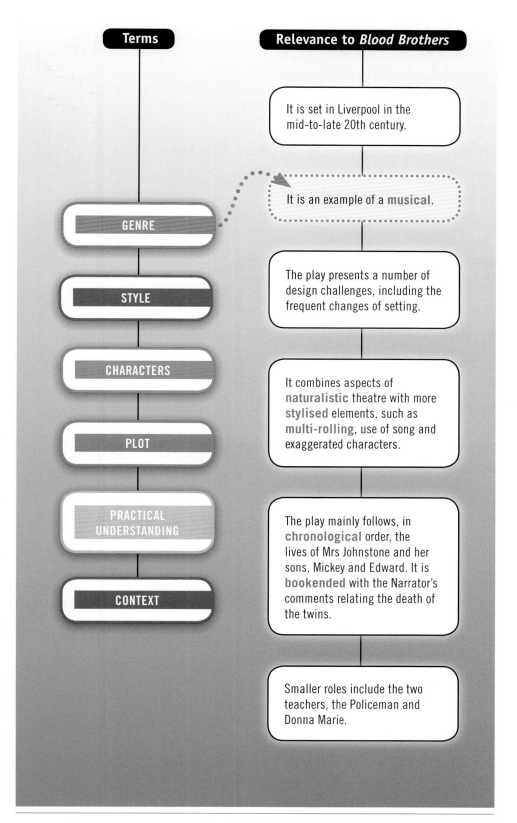

Terms

- GENRE
- STYLE
- CHARACTERS
- PLOT
- PRACTICAL UNDERSTANDING
- CONTEXT

Relevance to *Blood Brothers*

It is set in Liverpool in the mid-to-late 20th century.

It is an example of a **musical**.

The play presents a number of design challenges, including the frequent changes of setting.

It combines aspects of **naturalistic** theatre with more **stylised** elements, such as **multi-rolling**, use of song and exaggerated characters.

The play mainly follows, in **chronological** order, the lives of Mrs Johnstone and her sons, Mickey and Edward. It is **bookended** with the Narrator's comments relating the death of the twins.

Smaller roles include the two teachers, the Policeman and Donna Marie.

KEY TERMS

Musical: A type of play in which music, singing and dancing play a significant part.

Naturalistic: Lifelike, believable, realistic.

Stylised: Non-realistic, heightened, exaggerated.

Multi-rolling: When an actor plays more than one character (multiple roles).

Chronological: Events presented in the order in which they occurred.

Bookended: A structural device where the story ends at a similar point to where it began.

 TIP

As you study the play, make a note of the design challenges, particularly scene changes and the passing of time. Decide on practical design choices you could make to convey the plot and meaning of the play in order to make them clear and entertaining to the audience.

Plot: the sequence of the play's main events

ACT 1

Opening – Late 1950s / early 1960s

The Narrator introduces Mrs Johnstone and the play.

Mrs Johnstone is pregnant with twins.

Mrs Lyons convinces Mrs Johnstone to give up one of the twins.

The twins – Mickey and Edward – are born.

Mrs Lyons takes one of the twins.

Mrs Lyons fires Mrs Johnstone.

Seven years pass – 1960s

Mickey and Edward meet and become 'blood brothers'.

Mickey, Edward and Linda get into trouble with the police.

The Lyons decide to move away.

Edward comes to say goodbye and Mrs Johnstone gives him a locket.

The Johnstones are told they too are relocating.

INTERVAL: Seven years pass

Task B1

Explain three different ways in which you could show the passing of time in *Blood Brothers*.

Consider changes in:

- acting
- costume
- set
- lighting
- sound.

Provide specific examples of each specialism.

 TIP

You will never be asked just to describe the plot of the play. You must show an understanding of the play as a whole and your comprehension of how the events of the play affect the characters and the play's design.

ACT 2

Seven years later

Mrs Johnstone describes life in her new home.

Sammy gets into trouble for robbing a bus conductor.

Mickey and Linda attend a secondary modern school.

Edward attends a boarding school.

Mickey and Linda are suspended for being rude to a teacher.

Edward is suspended for not surrendering his locket to a teacher.

Linda and Mickey walk in a field and argue.

Mickey and Edward meet again and their friendship resumes.

Mrs Lyons attacks Mrs Johnstone.

CHECK IT OUT

For a complete synopsis of *Blood Brothers*, see pages 51–52 of *AQA GCSE Drama*.

Over several years – 1970s

Mickey, Edward and Linda become close friends.

Edward goes off to university.

Linda becomes pregnant.

Mickey and Linda marry.

Mickey is made redundant from his job in a box factory.

Edward returns from university and he and Mickey argue.

Mickey takes part in a robbery with Sammy and goes to prison.

Several years pass

Mickey comes out of prison; he is depressed and addicted to pills.

Edward is a councillor.

Linda and Edward start a relationship.

Mrs Lyons tells Mickey about the relationship.

Mickey interrupts a town council meeting to confront Edward.

Mickey shoots Edward.

The police shoot Mickey.

The Narrator brings the play to its conclusion.

Late 1970s / early 1980s

When did it happen?

✓ TEST YOURSELF B2

1 In which act do Linda and Mickey marry?

2 How much time passes between the first act of the play and the second?

3 How does Mrs Lyons convince Mrs Johnstone to give her one of the twins?

4 Who tells Mickey about Linda and Edward?

5 In which act do Mickey and Edward meet?

Task B2

Below are 12 key plot points from *Blood Brothers*. Put them in the order in which they occur in the play, numbering them 1 to 12.

When Mrs Lyons learns that Mrs Johnstone is expecting twins, she asks Mrs Johnstone to give one of the babies to her.

When seven-year-old Mickey meets Edward, they strike up an immediate friendship, becoming 'blood brothers'.

Sammy offers Mickey money to assist with a robbery, which results in Mickey going to prison.

Mrs Lyons attacks Mrs Johnstone because she believes she is following her and spoiling her relationship with Edward.

Linda and Mickey take a walk in a field, but Linda storms off when Mickey doesn't respond to her flirting.

Shortly after Linda and Mickey marry, he is made redundant.

The Narrator invites the audience to 'judge' Mrs Johnstone, the working-class mother of the twins.

Edward arrives at the Johnstone house to say goodbye and Mrs Johnstone gives him a locket with a photograph of Mickey in it.

Mickey and Edward die at the moment they learn that they are twins.

Mrs Johnstone sings about her past, explaining that by the age of 25 she had seven children and was expecting another.

Mrs Lyons sees Edward and Linda together and tells Mickey.

When Mrs Johnstone learns that they are being moved to a new area, she declares it a 'bright new day'.

Task B3

In your opinion, when is the play's climax?

Write three sentences to explain your choice.

KEY TERM

Climax: The moment of highest tension in a play, usually of great importance, and often the culmination of earlier events.

Who said that?

 TEST YOURSELF B3

Based on your reading of the play and your understanding of the main characters, match each line of dialogue with the correct character.

See if you can remember too in which act each line is spoken.

It's all right. I suppose, I suppose I always... loved you, in a way.

It's your work. Your work has deteriorated.

Edward... how would you like to move to another house?

Look... come on... I've got money, plenty of it.

But I've ironed him a shirt.

Come on, gang, let's go. We don't wanna play with these anyway. They're just kids.

I sometimes hate our Sammy.

Nothing! Nothing. (*Pause.*) You bought me off once before...

How they were born, and died, on the selfsame day.

God help the girls when you start dancing.

Take no notice, Mickey. I love you.

I could have been... I could have been him!

Where's me tablets gone, Linda?

So did y'hear the story of the Johnstone twins?

NARRATOR

LINDA

SAMMY

MRS LYONS

EDWARD

MRS JOHNSTONE

MICKEY

MR LYONS

Task B4

Locate the three lines spoken by Linda in Test yourself B3 and explain what the audience learns about her character from the things that she says.

 TIP

In the exam, you might be asked how you would use your vocal or physical skills to perform a single line. Look at the lines above and experiment with voice and movement choices that are appropriate for the character and their situation.

Key characters

You will need to demonstrate that you understand the characters in the play, including the different ways they could be interpreted and performed.

The descriptions below summarise the main characters in *Blood Brothers*.

MRS JOHNSTONE

- Working-class single mother.
- Works as a cleaner for Mrs Lyons.
- Expecting twins; afraid she won't be able to cope.
- Agrees to give up one of her twins, but regrets the decision.
- Raises Mickey, Sammy and her other children.
- Could be considered to be the play's **protagonist**.

SAMMY

- Mickey's older brother and the leader of their childhood gang.
- Bullies Mickey and misbehaves.
- As a teenager, begins committing crimes, including robbing a bus conductor.
- Convinces Mickey to take part in a robbery with him, where a man is shot.
- Mickey and he are sent to prison.

MICKEY

- The twin kept by Mrs Johnstone.
- At seven, a lively, friendly boy who is bullied by Sammy.
- Protected by his friend Linda.
- Meets Edward and becomes his friend; doesn't know they are twins.
- At 14, an awkward teenager, uninterested in school.
- Attracted to Linda, but unable to express his feelings.
- Friendship with Edward is important to him.
- After marrying Linda, he loses his job and is persuaded to commit a crime.
- After leaving prison, he is depressed and addicted to pills.

LINDA

- At seven, a confident girl, who is protective of Mickey.
- Unafraid to confront Sammy when he bullies Mickey.
- At 14, declares her love for Mickey and tries to get him to respond.
- Enjoys spending her teenage summers with Mickey and Edward.
- Linda is the **love interest** for both of the boys.

NARRATOR

- Mysterious, unnamed character.
- Comments on the action of the play.
- Reminds the audience that there are 'debts to pay' and there will be a 'reckoning day'.
- Could be considered a **choral character**.

MRS LYONS

- Middle-class married woman who employs Mrs Johnstone as a cleaner.
- Confesses her desire to have a child.
- Asks Mrs Johnstone to let her have one of the twins.
- Becomes worried about Mrs Johnstone coming between her and Edward.
- Mental health deteriorates.
- Attacks Mrs Johnstone with a knife.
- Tells Mickey about Edward and Linda's meetings.
- Could be considered the play's **antagonist**.

EDWARD

- Mickey's twin brother.
- Raised by the Lyons.
- At seven, a well-spoken, friendly boy eager to make new friends.
- Becomes 'blood brothers' with Mickey.
- Raised in a protective, middle-class environment.
- At 14, is sent to a boarding school.
- During teenage years, Mickey, Linda and he spend several summers together.
- Goes to university.
- Becomes a councillor and begins a relationship with Linda.

MR LYONS

- Mrs Lyons' husband.
- Has an important job which requires him to work long hours and travel.
- Exasperated by his wife's constant worrying.
- At his wife's urging, agrees to move the family out to the countryside.
- Seen firing employees in the song 'Take a Letter, Miss Jones'.

- Mickey finally asks her out and their relationship moves quickly.
- Becomes pregnant and marries Mickey.
- When Mickey comes out of prison, she asks Edward to help them.
- Begins seeing Edward secretly.

KEY TERMS

Protagonist: The leading character in a play.

Love interest: A character whose primary importance is their romantic relationship with a central character.

Choral character: A character who comments on the action of a play, while also participating in some of the action.

Antagonist: A character who opposes, works against or brings down the protagonist.

Blood Brothers in context

The context of a play includes the wider events, circumstances and influences of the period represented in the play:

▸ social

▸ historical

▸ political.

The characters in the play are affected by where they live, as well as the politics, economics and concerns of the time.

You will be expected to demonstrate how you could use the context of the play to influence design choices. An understanding of the context will also provide insight into the play's themes and the characters' feelings and motivations.

The first version of the play was performed in 1981 and the musical version in 1983. No specific dates are provided in the play, but the action is thought to span roughly from the late 1950s or early 1960s to the late 1970s or early 1980s.

Liverpool: history, society and culture

▸ The city was once a centre of industry with a thriving port which attracted workers from many regions, particularly Ireland and Wales.

▸ It was badly bombed during the Second World War.

▸ After the Second World War, particularly in the 1970s and 1980s, Liverpool's economy began to fail.

▸ Housing for poorer communities was built in redeveloped areas of the city, as well as in outer areas like Skelmersdale.

▸ Some inhabitants of poorer inner-city areas were rehoused to these outer areas.

▸ In the 1960s and 1970s, Liverpool was particularly associated with youth culture and the thriving music scene.

Education

▸ Students in state education took a test called the '11-plus' which determined what type of secondary school they would attend: either a grammar school (if they passed) or a secondary modern (if they didn't).

▸ Secondary modern schools were designed for children who were assessed by the 11-plus exam to have less academic potential than those who could attend a grammar school.

▸ Private-school students might attend fee-paying schools either as a day student (which meant they still lived at home) or as a boarder at a boarding school (where they lived at the school during term time).

▸ Children from middle-class backgrounds were much more likely to go to grammar or private schools than working-class children.

▸ Students from grammar schools or private schools were more likely to go on to university than students from secondary modern schools.

Unemployment

▸ In the 1970s, many factories and businesses in Liverpool closed.

▸ Liverpool became an area of particularly high unemployment.

▸ The working class was hit hard by the loss of jobs in factories and on the docks.

▸ 'Being on the dole' meant that you were out of work and receiving unemployment support or other benefits.

Women's roles

Housewives in Liverpool, 1962 ▲

▸ In the 1960s, there were some improvements in women's rights, including, for example, movement towards equal pay which was partly prompted by successful strikes such as that at the Ford factory in Dagenham in 1968.

▸ In 1975, the Sex Discrimination Act was passed which was intended to eliminate sex discrimination in employment and to provide equal opportunities for men and women.

▸ Attitudes to women's roles did not universally change, however. A UK survey in 1984 showed that almost half of those who answered felt that it was a man's job to earn money and a woman's job to look after the home.

▸ The role of wife and mother was considered the most important to many. It was still a common assumption that a woman would stay at home once she had children.

▸ Marilyn Monroe (1926–62), a Hollywood film star who is referred to in the play, was considered a feminine ideal to many due to her beauty and sexual appeal.

The theme of social class

One of the important themes of *Blood Brothers* is social class. The economic recession of the 1970s hit working-class families particularly hard. By the early 1980s, a Liverpool MP reported to Parliament that one in every five Liverpool families was on benefits and in some poorer areas as much as half of the working population was unemployed. Middle-class families, such as the Lyons, generally weathered the economic setbacks with more ease. Although the houses of different social classes might be near each other, they would often lead very different lives, from the types of school they attended, to how much money they had to spend on clothing, food or luxury items.

An unemployment protest at the Tate and Lyle factory in Liverpool, 1976 ▲

 TEST YOURSELF B4

From your understanding of the play and the contexts described here, answer the following questions:

1 Whose new address is going to be 65 Skelmerdsale Lane?

2 Who goes on the dole?

3 Who attends a secondary modern school?

4 Who attends a boarding school?

5 Who goes to university?

6 Who dictates a letter firing workers?

7 Who earns the money in the Lyons household?

8 What opportunities does Edward have that Mickey doesn't?

Task B5

Locate three incidents in the play that show the differences between Edward's and Mickey's lives, including the opportunities they have.

Write three to five sentences explaining how you could use the play's social context to emphasise the differences.

Consider, for example:

• costume

• hair and make-up

• set design

• acting techniques.

CHECK IT OUT

For more on the context of *Blood Brothers*, see page 53 of *AQA GCSE Drama*.

Willy Russell and the contexts behind his playwriting

The award-winning playwright, Willy Russell is known for many popular plays including *Educating Rita* and *Shirley Valentine* as well as *Blood Brothers*. He is widely admired for his insightful portrayals of working-class characters, in particular, strong, independent-minded women, and for his exploration of themes such as social class and education.

The following are excerpts from an interview that Angela Levin conducted with Willy Russell for the *Telegraph* newspaper in 2012.

Task B6

Re-read the excerpts from the interview and highlight points that you think are relevant to *Blood Brothers*.

Then answer these questions.

1 Where did Willy Russell grow up?

2 What similarities are there between his life and the characters in *Blood Brothers*?

3 What inspired him to write *Blood Brothers*?

4 Russell is admired for his sympathetic portrayal of strong female characters. What in his background might have inspired this?

Willy Russell: 'I want to talk about things that matter'

[Willy Russell's] own story is as powerful as any fiction. An only child, he was born in Whiston, near Liverpool, to a working-class couple who had little in common. 'It was a phenomenally tense situation at home because my parents wanted different things from life,' he recalls...

He believes that spending so much time with his mother, aunts and grandmother developed his understanding of women and of how to write convincing female characters.

'When I was 11 I was at quite a rough school, but we used to read one-act plays, and one about two babies switched at birth stayed with me. I thought a lot about what might happen to each of them, and it became the seed for *Blood Brothers*. (Please write that it absolutely isn't based on the 1844 novella *The Corsican Brothers* by Alexandre Dumas, as written in Wikipedia!)'

'I am very interested in nature versus nurture. When I look at myself or catch sight of a gesture I make and see my father... I also know I might have drunk myself to death at 30. Luckily, I was saved by my in-laws, who nurtured me.'

Russell left school at 15 with one O-level in English literature and, at his mother's suggestion, became a hairdresser. He also wrote songs and set up a group...

'Meeting Annie's [his wife's] family was a massive influence in my life. One day her mother Margaret, who knew I hated hairdressing, said if I didn't want to do it all my life, what was I going to do about it? I said I wanted to teach because I could then write in the holidays. She explained that I needed five O-levels, and suggested I went to night school. I was 20 and took her advice.'

Russell became a teacher in Toxteth, but within a year was writing full time...

Jodie Prenger in Shirley Valentine ▲

Costumes that reflect context

Costumes are an important design element of a drama production. They influence the audience's perception of the characters, the time period and the physical setting.

If you are asked about costumes in the exam, you will need to offer design ideas that show evidence of the context of the play, such as the working-class community of Liverpool in the 1960s and 1970s.

When designing a costume, you might consider:

▶ Style, cut and fit
▶ Colour, fabric, decorative features (buttons, trim, ribbons and so on)
▶ Condition (worn or new, neat or wrinkled, clean or stained and so on)
▶ Footwear
▶ Headgear
▶ Accessories
▶ Make-up and hairstyle.

When creating these, you need to bear in mind the **status**, occupation and social role of the character. These will influence how the character looks, and they are also attributes of the character that you need to put across to the audience.

> **KEY TERM**
>
> **Status:** The social or professional standing of a character.

Costumes for Mrs Johnstone and Mrs Lyons

A scene from *Cathy Come Home*, a 1966 television film about a struggling low-income family ▲

1960s women with sufficient disposable income to enjoy eating out ▲

Task B7

Study these photographs and think about how they might inspire designs for Mrs Johnstone and Mrs Lyons. Draw quick sketches of your ideas.

Remember that the costumes should reflect the play's contexts.

Task B8

Look at the list below of ideas for costume, make-up and hairstyles. Given your understanding of the characters and their roles, label which ones are best for Mrs Johnstone and which for Mrs Lyons.

Hair curled and styled, set with hairspray

A cashmere twin-set

Low-heeled, scuffed work shoes

Yellow washing-up gloves

A loose jumper with rolled-up sleeves

Hair loosely tied back and unstyled

Red lipstick

High-heeled, patent leather shoes

A feather duster

A knee-length tweed skirt

Leather gloves

A polyester, tabard-style apron

A string of pearls

Costumes for Mickey, Edward and Linda, aged 7 and 14

Task B9

The costumes for Linda, Mickey and Edward at age 7 should reflect their backgrounds. Look at these notes about costumes for the children at this age and decide which of the three children is being described.

Note what the costume reveals about each character and how it reflects the context.

- Baggy hand-me-down shorts, patched and held up with a belt.
- An over-sized striped jumper with holes in it.
- Rumpled, loose socks and heavy black shoes with white laces.
- Mud on knees.
- Hair a little too long and sticking up.

- A short dress, with stains and some rips, worn over baggy cotton shorts.
- Ankle socks and T-strap shoes.
- Hair up in bunches.
- A smudge of dirt on cheek.

- Neat grey shorts with a crease ironed into them.
- Short-sleeved white shirt, well-pressed and very clean.
- A grey sleeveless pullover with a thin orange stripe at the bottom.
- Grey socks, neatly pulled up to mid-calf.
- Short hair, smoothly parted to the side.

Task B10

Between Act 1 and Act 2, seven years pass. The actors, including those playing Linda, Mickey and Edward, have the interval to change costume, hair and make-up.

Consider the following contextual information and then sketch your costume designs.

- The characters are now 14.
- They are interested in being attractive.
- At school, they might have to wear a uniform.
- For their leisure outfits, they might be influenced by celebrities of the time.
- They might be influenced by magazines and other fashion guides of the time.
- They might have limited money to spend on their clothing.

TIP

Remember that you can discuss hair and make-up, as well as accessories such as jewellery, scarves and bags, when creating your costume design.

LOOK HERE

For more ideas on how to write about costumes, go to page 73.

Task B11

Choose one of the following characters and describe or sketch your ideas for their costume in Act 2. Add notes on what the costume indicates about character and context.

- Sammy
- Mr Lyons
- The Narrator.

How the play's context might be shown in set and prop design

Another specialism you might be asked to refer to when discussing the context of a particular extract is the set, which could include stage furnishings and **props**.

Your ideas will need to take into account the social contexts of the play, such as the working-class community of Liverpool in the 1970s.

Set design

When designing a set, you might consider:

▶ Stage configuration (proscenium, in the round, end on and so on)
▶ A **composite set** or a number of different sets, which will need to be changed to suit the different locations
▶ The scale (how large) your set will be
▶ Any levels/platforms, ramps or stairs
▶ Locations of the actors' entrances and exits
▶ Any backdrops, flats or projections
▶ The colours, textures and shapes used
▶ Any necessary props, **set dressings** or furnishings.

Domestic interior

> **KEY TERMS**
>
> **Props:** Small items that actors can carry, such as books, a hairbrush, a package or a mug.
>
> **Composite set:** A single set that represents several locations at once.
>
> **Set dressings:** Items on the set not actually used as props, but that create detail and interest in it, such as vases or framed paintings on a wall.

Task B12

Look at the photographs below, taken in roughly the same period, and decide which is more suitable for the Lyons' home and which for the Johnstones', and why.

A

B

Work with a study partner to discuss the different lifestyles suggested by each photograph.

Task B14

From your knowledge of the play, as well as any extra research you have undertaken, list at least four props, set dressings or furnishings that could be used in the interior for a set design for the Johnstone home and for the Lyons home.

For each item, write one sentence explaining what it shows about the characters and their social and economic context. Use a table like this one to help you.

Johnstone home	Lyons home
Item: *Furniture: a highchair*	Item: *Books*
Explanation: *Mrs Johnstone has many babies in a short period of time, so there is a highchair in constant use.*	Explanation: *The Lyons value learning and Edward is used to reading and using reference books, so there would be books easily available in the house.*
Item:	Item:
Explanation:	Explanation:

> **KEY TERMS**
>
> **Truck:** A platform on wheels upon which scenery can be mounted and moved.
>
> **Ensemble:** A group of actors. In some productions, ensemble members might play additional small roles and/or act as a chorus.

Rural exterior

The following is a student-style response explaining set-design ideas for the field scene in Act 2 of *Blood Brothers* (pages 70–71). Note the annotations.

① Identifies type of stage configuration and use of projection.

② Understands context of scene within the play.

③ Notes historical and social context.

④ Uses correct terminology ('truck') and shows understanding of how theatre is created.

⑤ Indicates best stage location for the item of set.

⑥ Suggests how the set can contribute to mood and style.

I would set this scene on a thrust stage and use a projection on the upstage flat to show a large field. ① This should contrast with the urban locations of the other scenes ②, so I want to emphasise its unfamiliar green and naturalness. Linda and Mickey are city-dwellers transplanted to this surprising environment, as was happening to many Liverpool residents at this time. ③

I would have the Narrator push a truck ④ carrying a wooden stile to place upstage right ⑤ for Linda and Mickey to clamber over. The stile will be a rugged one, not frequently used, suggesting that they might be trespassing. It will also highlight the comedy ⑥ of the scene as Linda pretends she can't get over it in order to force Mickey to make physical contact with her.

Ensemble members will roll out green artificial carpets of grass around the edges of the thrust stage to further emphasise the unusual setting and add more humour, by acting as though it is a competitive game, with one person correcting how someone else has done it.

School interior

Task B15

Read pages 66–67 of *Blood Brothers*, from 'As Edward exits…' to 'Linda and Mickey leave the class.' Look closely at the stage direction:

> A class in a secondary modern school is formed – all boredom and futility.

Write a paragraph describing a set design for this school scene which reinforces the stage direction and demonstrates your understanding of the play's context.

 **LOOK HERE**

For more ideas about how to write about sets, including technical terminology, go to pages 106–111 in Section C.

The ending

Task B15

1   Imagine you have been asked to create a set design for the ending of the play (from page 104, 'Edward: And if, for once…' to the end).
    Choose one of the following staging configurations:
    - traverse
    - end on
    - theatre in the round.

2   Draw a sketch of the design indicating:
    - Where entrances and exits will occur
    - Where the audience is seated in relation to the stage
    - How you will make clear where the action is taking place (the scene's setting)
    - The colours, textures and materials used in your design.

3   Write a paragraph and/or annotations around your sketch to explain how your design will support the action of the ending of the play and is appropriate to the play's context.

How lighting and sound contribute to context

Other design specialisms which you might be asked to discuss in relation to the play's context include lighting and sound. Your design ideas for either must reflect the social, economic, historical or cultural circumstances of the characters and their setting, such as the working-class community of Liverpool in the 1960s or 1970s.

This might seem more challenging than designing either costumes or a set, which could more easily be based on photographs and other research about Liverpool and the time period, so you will need to be imaginative in the ways that the sound or lighting could suggest the period, location and/or social message.

Lighting

When creating a lighting design, you might think about:

> Angles and intensity

> Special effects

> Transitions, such as the use of blackouts or fades.

> Light from onstage sources, such as standard lamps

> Use of shadow and silhouette

In order to suggest the context of *Blood Brothers*, you might use lighting to:

▸ suggest the location of a scene

▸ highlight differences between the social classes

▸ indicate the time period of the scene

▸ create an atmosphere or mood of a scene in relation to the play's themes.

Task B16

Read these quotes by theatre makers and identify:

- Where in *Blood Brothers* the lighting idea might be effective
- How it demonstrates the context of the play.

> In the transition, I would have a flickering white light projected on the upstage flat, suggesting the fleeting images of the film Mickey and Eddie have been watching.

> For the fairground, I would use a swirling gobo to suggest a Ferris wheel nearby. I would have a red neon sign that says 'Wong's Chinese Food' which would abruptly be turned off.

> To contrast the happiness of the wedding with the despair of being fired, I would use a very different colour palette for the lighting. I would have it fade from rosy and golden hues to dull grey tones. Mr Lyons and Miss Jones will be spot-lit to show that they are separate from the 'Dole-ites', until Miss Jones is shown unhappily joining the grey-lit group of the unemployed when she too is fired.

KEY TERMS

Gobo: A metal cut-out used to project patterns, such as leaves, stars, swirls or waves.

Colour palette: The range of colours used. For example, a scene might use light colours, dark colours, muted tones, grey tones, earth tones or vivid, primary colours.

Task B17

Read pages 77–79, from 'As they run off, we see Mrs Lyons' to 'Kids' voices are heard, chanting, off'. Make notes on any moments of the scene that stand out as being suitable for a particular lighting design.

1   Consider how you could use lighting to achieve the following:
   - An emphasis that, at the beginning of the scene, Mrs Lyons is emerging from a dark, hidden place
   - That Mrs Johnstone's kitchen is a cheery, simple working-class space
   - The mood changes dramatically when Mrs Lyons attacks Mrs Johnstone
   - That Mrs Johnstone is shaken and upset at the end of the scene.
2   Now read the beginning of a sample response about using lighting to establish context in this scene. Complete the response with your own ideas about how lighting could support the action of the scene and show the play's context.

> I want to show that Mrs Lyons and Mrs Johnstone have, in some ways, changed places. At the beginning of the play Mrs Johnstone had a higher status, but Mrs Johnstone is, at this point, despite her relative poverty, the happier person...

Task B19

Look closely at page 37 of *Blood Brothers*, from 'The scene fades...' to '...unnoticed by the battling children.'

How could you use sound design to show the Liverpool working-class community in this scene?

LOOK HERE

Go to page 74 to learn more terminology for writing about lighting and sound.

Sound

- When creating a sound design, you might consider using:
- Live or recorded sound
- Sound effects or music
- Volume and means of amplification
- Particular sources of sound or directions of sound.

Task B18

Here are some effects a sound designer would like to achieve. Write down your ideas on how they could go about creating these effects to reflect the play's context. An example has been suggested to start you off.

A   I want to show how music was important to Liverpool teenagers at this time.

Sound: *When Mickey is first seen at the beginning of Act 2 in his room, I would have loud rock music playing and he could play an air guitar to it. The music will be over-amplified from speakers around the audience, so it is as if the audience is in Mickey's room. As soon as his mother speaks, the music will snap off, as if she has intruded on his private world.*

B   I want to create the atmosphere and sounds of a 1970s bus.

C   I want to show the innocence of the teenage Liverpool summers of Mickey, Edward and Linda.

D   After he loses his job, I want to show Mickey's nervousness and despair during the robbery.

Exam-style example question: Component 1, Section B, Question 1

The first question in Section B will focus on the context of the play and an element of design, in relation to a specific extract from the play. Below are several sample questions.

A Focus on Act 1, pages 42–43, from 'Linda: An' listen Mickey…' to '*They all laugh.*'

You are designing a costume for Linda to wear in a performance of this extract. The costume must reflect the context of *Blood Brothers*, set in a working-class community in the period of the 1970s. Describe your design ideas for the costume. [4 marks]

B Focus on Act 1, page 8, from 'Mrs Lyons: Hello, Mrs Johnstone, how are you?' to 'Mrs Lyons begins to unwrap her parcel.'

You are designing a setting for a performance of this extract. The setting must reflect the context of *Blood Brothers* set in Liverpool in the period between the 1960s and the 1980s. [4 marks]

C Focus on Act 2, page 99, from 'Mickey and Linda are in their new house' to 'Linda: You promised.'

You are designing props or items of furniture for a performance of this extract. The props or items of furniture must reflect the context of *Blood Brothers*, set in a working-class community around the 1970s. Describe your ideas for props or items of furniture. [4 marks]

D Focus on Act 2, page 82, from 'Linda, Mickey and Edward pool their money…' to 'At the midnight hour, at seventeen.'

You are designing the lighting for a performance of this extract. The lighting must reflect the context of *Blood Brothers*, set in a working-class community in the 1970s. Describe your ideas for the lighting. [4 marks]

E Focus on Act 2, pages 103–104, from 'As the music abruptly segues' to 'Linda: Mam… Mam… what's…'

You are designing the sound for a performance of this extract. The sound must reflect the context of *Blood Brothers*, set in Liverpool in the late 1970s. Describe your ideas for the sound. [4 marks]

Task B21

For each extract specified in the sample questions, write two more exam-style questions of your own. Use the same style as those above, but focus on different design elements.

TIP

Be aware of the number of marks available for a question in the exam. For questions worth relatively few marks, avoid spending too long writing. Instead, try to write accurately and concisely. For the questions here – each worth four marks – you can score highly with just a single, well-developed paragraph.

Task B20

For each of the exam-style questions on this page, plan a response. Make sure that you include:

• How your design shows the context
• How your design is appropriate for the extract
• Precise details of your design.

LOOK HERE

For more ideas on how to practise your exam writing skills, go to page 124.

Sample answers for Component 1, Section B, Question 1

Task B22

On the right are two extracts from different student-style responses to the same question. Read them through and highlight or annotate them.

- Next to every mention of **context**, write **C**.
- Next to each precise **design** detail, write **D**.
- Next to every point which shows **understanding** of the play and character, write **U**.

TIP

There is not just one correct answer for questions like this. As long as a response is based on an excellent understanding of the play and its context and gives precise details of how design could be used to create appropriate effects, it can gain high marks.

KEY TERM

Affluent: Wealthy, prosperous, well off.

Focus on Act 2, pages 77–78, from 'As they run off' to 'Mrs Johnstone: He is yours.'

You are designing a costume for Mrs Lyons for a performance of this extract. The costume must reflect the context of *Blood Brothers*, set in a working-class community during the 1970s. Describe your ideas for the costume.

[4 marks]

Earlier in the play, we saw Mrs Lyons as a neat, affluent middle-class woman. Although her costume in this extract will still reflect clothing that a woman of her status in 1970s Liverpool would choose, there will also be signs of her deteriorating mental health. As she has been 'concealed' in an alley, I would have her wearing a dark-patterned silk headscarf that women often wore during this time to protect their hair from wind and rain. She will also have a good-quality, belted trench coat on over her well-made, conservative woollen dress, suitable for her affluent background. The plain coat will show that she doesn't want to stand out in this unfamiliar neighbourhood. In Mrs Johnstone's kitchen, she will take off the headscarf, revealing that her hair is untidy. She will be wearing less make-up than in earlier scenes. This will help to indicate that she is beginning to lose control.

Task B23

Now write your own response to a costume design for the same extract, but this time focus on a costume for Mrs Johnstone.

Afterwards, check that you have:
- Related it to the play's context
- Provided precise details of the costume
- Shown an understanding of the character and play.

Mrs Lyons will wear a dark, knee-length tweed skirt and a black, cashmere, long-sleeved jumper. Over this outfit, she will have a loosely belted black coat. These items of clothing are appropriate for a middle-class woman in 1970s Liverpool and for the chilly weather, but the dark colours also suggest her darker mood. This will contrast with the brighter colours of Mrs Johnstone. Mrs Lyons will wear dark-red lipstick, which will look like a gash across her face and hint at her later violence. Her hair will be tightly curled, but not fashionable. It will show that she hasn't moved with the times. She will wear dark leather gloves, which she keeps on, indicating that she doesn't plan to stay long and lending her a menacing appearance.

Characterisation

You need to understand how different roles in the play could be performed. The playwright has given indications about the characters and their backgrounds, feelings and desires. Actors and directors must use their skills to convey these ideas to the audience.

Areas to consider when developing a performance include:

▸ The character's importance to the play
▸ Whether the character changes and develops during the play
▸ In what ways an actor could use vocal and physical skills to portray the character
▸ How an actor could use the stage space and interaction with others
▸ How the play's context and style might influence acting choices
▸ What the character's thoughts, feelings and **motivations** are and how these might be put across or influence acting choices
▸ How the **subtext** of the character's lines could be expressed
▸ What impact the actor's choices would have on how the audience understands the character.

KEY TERMS

Motivations: The feelings behind what a character wants or needs, in a particular scene.

Subtext: The unspoken meaning, feelings and thoughts 'beneath' the lines, which might be shown in the characters' body language, tone of voice and facial expressions.

TEST YOURSELF B5

The following simple descriptions of characters from *Blood Brothers* indicate some of the important features that need to be considered when developing characterisations. Match each one with the correct character's name.

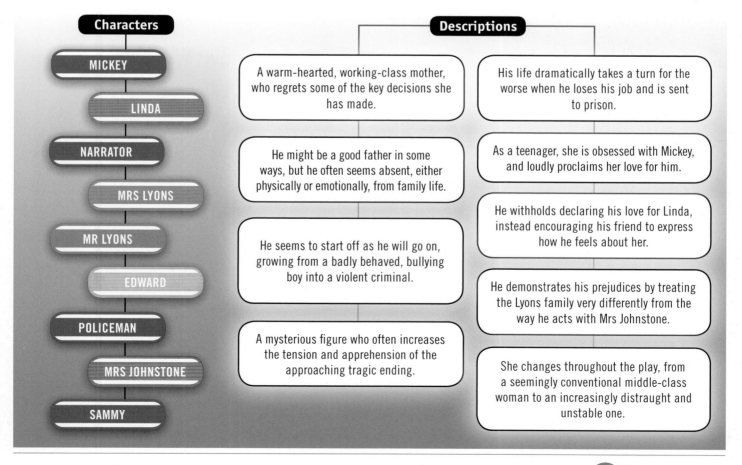

Characters

MICKEY

LINDA

NARRATOR

MRS LYONS

MR LYONS

EDWARD

POLICEMAN

MRS JOHNSTONE

SAMMY

Descriptions

A warm-hearted, working-class mother, who regrets some of the key decisions she has made.

His life dramatically takes a turn for the worse when he loses his job and is sent to prison.

He might be a good father in some ways, but he often seems absent, either physically or emotionally, from family life.

As a teenager, she is obsessed with Mickey, and loudly proclaims her love for him.

He seems to start off as he will go on, growing from a badly behaved, bullying boy into a violent criminal.

He withholds declaring his love for Linda, instead encouraging his friend to express how he feels about her.

He demonstrates his prejudices by treating the Lyons family very differently from the way he acts with Mrs Johnstone.

A mysterious figure who often increases the tension and apprehension of the approaching tragic ending.

She changes throughout the play, from a seemingly conventional middle-class woman to an increasingly distraught and unstable one.

KEY TERMS

Nature versus nurture: An area of debate that seeks to determine if there are genetic and biological issues (nature) that determine a person's characteristics and behaviour or whether environmental issues, including home life and education (nurture) are more important. The study of identical twins separated at birth is important in this area of sociology, as twins are as close as two people can be in terms of genetics, but, in these cases, are raised in different environments.

Received pronunciation (RP): A way of speaking that is considered the 'standard' form of English pronunciation. It is associated with education and formal speaking.

Dramatic irony: When the audience knows something that one or more characters on stage do not.

Characterisation focus on Mickey and Edward

Mickey and Edward, and their similarities and differences, are at the heart of *Blood Brothers*. By using twins separated soon after birth, Willy Russell's play directly asks the question about whether our fate is determined by our upbringing, which is part of the **nature versus nurture** debate.

Task B24

What are the similarities and differences between Mickey and Edward?

Look at the statements below. If a statement is true only for Mickey, put it in his section of a Venn diagram. If a statement is true just for Edward, put it in his section. For any statement true of both boys, put it in the overlapping section.

Is in love with Linda.
Is working class.
Has a sense of humour.
Speaks in a Liverpool dialect.
Mrs Johnstone is their birth mother.
Raised by Mrs Lyons.
Goes to a secondary modern school.
Loses his job in the box factory.
Goes to prison.
Dies at the end of the play.

Is middle class.
Speaks with **received pronunciation** (or another middle-class dialect).
Raised by Mrs Johnstone.
Attends a private boarding school.
Is a twin.
Enjoys teenage summers with Linda.
Goes to university.

Mickey   Is in love with Linda.   Edward

Differences and misunderstandings

A significant element of the comedy in the first meeting between Mickey and Edward derives from the differences between the two characters and their misunderstandings of each other. Although the audience is aware that they are twins, the boys are not. This is an example of **dramatic irony**. If you were performing as Mickey or Edward, you would need to consider how you might emphasise the differences between them.

Task B25

With a partner, read the scene when the boys first meet at the age of seven, from 'Edward, also seven appears' to 'Mickey: (*taking a handful*) Are you soft?' Then work together to complete the following activities:

1 Edward is described as 'bright and forthcoming', whereas Mickey greets him 'suspiciously'. Create a **still image** showing the postures, facial expressions and stage positioning of the two boys when they first meet.

2 What are the characters' motivations in this scene? Why does Edward approach Mickey? Why does Mickey continue to speak to him?

3 Experiment with the use of **dialect**. How might the boys' word choices and way of speaking be different? How do these differences contribute to the comedy?

4 Why is Mickey shocked when Edward agrees to give him a sweet? How might the actor use his voice and body language to express this shock?

5 Experiment with **pace** in the scene. When do you think the characters would answer each other quickly and when might there be pauses?

6 How might the actor playing Edward use his voice and physical skills to show that he doesn't mind giving away his sweets? Experiment with pace, volume, facial expression and gesture to convey Edward's innocence and openness.

7 Experiment with saying the line 'Are you soft?' in the following ways:
   • Quickly, while grabbing a handful of sweets, before Edward can change his mind
   • Quietly, as if sharing a secret, and taking and hiding the sweets before anyone else sees them
   • Loudly, with a matter-of-fact tone, while casually helping himself to more sweets.

KEY TERMS

Still image: An acting technique when you freeze a moment in silence, showing the characters' positions and facial expressions.

Dialect: A way of speaking that is specific to a certain location or social group.

Pace: The speed or rate at which something happens.

Task B26

Use the grids below to note the vocal and physical qualities of Mickey and Edward as teenagers and young men. Give at least one precise example when these traits might be noticeable. A few suggestions have been made to get you started.

As teenagers	Mickey	Edward
Posture		
Gestures		Awkward when his mother is teaching him to dance, holding his arms out stiffly as he clumsily tries to remember the steps.
Facial expressions	Avoids eye contact and looks down, embarrassed, as his mother teases him about Linda.	
Vocal volume/pace		
Vocal tone		

As adults	Mickey	Edward
Posture		
Gestures		
Facial expressions		
Vocal volume/pace	Speaks slowly and quietly in most of the pill scene with Linda, due to his depression and use of sedatives.	
Vocal tone		Tries to hide his fear when Mickey appears with a gun by speaking gently and evenly.

Characterisation focus on Mrs Lyons and Mrs Johnstone

Feelings and motivations

Mrs Lyons and Mrs Johnstone are two characters whose feelings and motivations are often at odds.

Mrs Lyons' desire for a child is so strong that she is willing to trample over Mrs Johnstone's feelings. Through a combination of threats and manipulation, she insists that Mrs Johnstone relinquish all contact with Edward.

Mrs Johnstone fears losing her other children and is superstitious about what will happen if the boys know each other's identity. She does, however, rebel against Mrs Lyons' wishes at times, such as when she gives Edward the locket or when she doesn't discourage the teenage friendship between the boys.

Similarities and differences

Task B27

Look at these descriptive adjectives and decide if they best describe Mrs Johnstone, Mrs Lyons or both.

Affectionate

Resourceful

Optimistic

Protective

Manipulative

Amusing

Superstitious

Obsessed

Single mother

Good-humoured

Fearful

Unstable

Middle class

Sympathetic

Married

Working class

Task B28

Read pages 18–19, when Mrs Lyons comes to take the infant Edward. Mrs Lyons' initial motivation is to take one of the babies, and Mrs Johnstone's is to delay or prevent this.

1　As Mrs Lyons, experiment with the following different subtexts in the line 'They're born, you didn't notify me.':

　A　You have heard that the babies were born and are angry that Mrs Johnstone didn't tell you.

　B　You are nervous that Mrs Johnstone will change her mind so don't want to frighten her.

　C　You want to remind Mrs Johnstone of her obligation to you and to assert your dominance as her employer.

2　How did the different subtexts affect your voice? Choose the delivery that you found most effective and make notes on:

　●　Volume　　●　Tone

　●　Pace　　●　Emphasis on certain words.

3　As a performer playing Mrs Johnstone, how would you use your voice to reply? Experiment with her line 'Well, I... I just... it's... couldn't I keep them for a few more days, please, please, they're a pair, they go together.' Try the following:

　A　You are trying to delay and avoid giving Mrs Lyons one of the babies.

　B　You feel depressed and are resigned to giving up one of the babies.

　C　You are emotional and desperate to keep both of the babies.

4　How did the different subtexts affect your voice? Again, write about the delivery that you thought was most effective and why.

5　Now, looking specifically at Mrs Johnstone's line You'd better... 'You'd better see which one you want,' write a response to the following exam-style question:

　You are performing the role of Mrs Johnstone.

　Describe how you would use your vocal and physical skills to perform this line. Explain the effects you wish to create.

Task B29

Complete the following grid, showing acting skills at key points in the play. Some ideas have been suggested for you.

Consider the following vocal and physical skills each time:

●　Accent/dialect　　●　Pauses and pace　　●　Gestures　　●　Tone

●　Volume　　●　Gait and posture　　●　Facial expressions.

Scene/pages	Mrs Johnstone	Mrs Lyons
8–9: Mrs Lyons explains that they haven't been able to have children	Vocal skills: *Cheerful. Liverpool working-class dialect. Speaks respectfully to her employer.* Physical skills:	Vocal skills: *Confident, friendly tone. Received pronunciation.* *Tone of voice is sadder and slower when she explains that she is afraid they can never have children.* Physical skills:
22: Mrs Lyons accuses Mrs Johnstone of selling her baby	Vocal skills: Physical skills:	Vocal skills: Physical skills:
78: Mrs Lyons tries to pay Mrs Johnstone to move away	Vocal skills: Physical skills:	Vocal skills: Physical skills:

Characterisation focus on Linda and Sammy

Although Linda and Sammy are both strong characters, raised in similar environments, their personalities are very different. From the beginning, Sammy is shown to be a bully, whereas Linda is protective.

Task B30

Use the grid below to explain the motivations of Sammy and Linda in these scenes where they come into conflict.

Scene	What Linda wants	What Sammy wants
Page 41: Linda tells Sammy he will go to hell with Mickey	*To protect Mickey.*	
Page 64: Sammy robs the bus conductor		
Page 95: Mickey says he will be back later to take Linda out		

 Linda

Task B31

1 The performer playing Linda will have to show how she changes through her life. Look at the descriptions below and decide if you think these vocal and physical choices would better suit Linda at 7, 14 or in her 20s.

I would play Linda as a confident, flirtatious person who knows how attractive she is. I will be playful and expressive, joking, pulling faces and doing silly poses. I will frequently laugh and grab hold of Mickey and Edward. Linda is forthright, so I will speak loudly and quickly.

I would play Linda as someone who has to be more mature than her years. I will have a motherly manner, taking Mickey's arm, gently coaxing him to take his lunch and get to work on time. I am still protecting him and so speak softly and soothingly. I will avoid direct eye contact when Mickey gets angry.

I see Linda as someone who is athletic and confident. I would stand with my legs wide and hands on my hips, in defiance of Sammy. I would use forceful gestures, such as pointing angrily. When I think I have outwitted him, I will laugh and nod as if to say 'so there'. My voice is loud with a Liverpool accent.

2 Look at the following lines and explain how an actor playing Linda could create certain effects.

Linda's line	Desired effect	Vocal skills to use	Physical skills to use
Page 71: Well, he is. An' what do you care if I think another boy's gorgeous, eh?			
Page 98: I get depressed but I don't take those. You don't need those, Mickey.			

Sammy

Sammy is a **volatile** figure. He is a source of comedy in the play's first act. In the second act, he is a source of danger and involves Mickey in a crime.

KEY TERM

Volatile: Likely to change suddenly; explosive; unpredictable.

Task B32

1   Experiment with the following lines for Sammy and then describe how you could use vocal and physical skills to create **comic** effects.

> I'm gonna do another burial. Me worms have died again. (page 32)
>
> Cos when we swear... we cross our fingers. (page 41)

2   Now try the following lines, experimenting with how you could use vocal and physical skills to create **frightening** or **menacing** effects.

> I'm not defraudin' no one. (page 64)
>
> We don't use the shooters. They're just frighteners. (page 93)

 TIP

Keep in mind how the characters change and develop throughout the play. The effect you want to create in a particular scene will depend on what has happened before as well as what is happening during the extract presented.

KEY TERMS

Symbolic: Using something to represent something else. For example, the Narrator might be a figure who symbolises the unemployed of Liverpool.

Pitch: How high or low a voice is.

Intonation: The rise and fall of pitch in the voice; the musicality of speech.

Phrasing: How the words in a line of speech are grouped together. For example, whether a line is said on a single breath or broken into fragments.

Register: The vocal range of the voice (upper, middle or lower register) and the variety of tones of voice.

Characterisation focus on Mr Lyons and the Narrator

Mr Lyons and the Narrator are very different characters. Mr Lyons is usually played naturalistically, as a believable middle-class husband and businessman.

The Narrator serves a more **symbolic** role, as a bridge between the audience and the action of the play. Most of his lines are either rhyming poetry or songs. Occasionally, he might be called on to multi-role as other minor characters in the play.

 Mr Lyons

Task B33

Look at Mr Lyons' lines below and identify:
* The context of the line (what is happening shortly before it)
* His motivations for saying the line
* The impact of the line on the audience.
    * **A** Ask Mummy. Darling, I'll see you later now. Must dash. (page 34)
    * **B** Jennifer, Jennifer, how many times... the factory is here, my work is here... (page 44)
    * **C** A most miserable sign of the times. (page 89)

 The Narrator

Task B34

1 Read the following description of the possible ways an actor could use vocal skills to express the Narrator's role in his opening speech. Find examples of: volume, **pitch**, timing/pace, **intonation**, **phrasing**, emotional range.

At the opening of the play, I would speak in a lower **register**, which will sound commanding and establish the Narrator as a powerful character. I would say the word 'So' loudly and in a confrontational manner, which should surprise the audience.

I will pause slightly before beginning the next line as the Narrator is describing a situation going from bad to worse.

My tone will change on the phrase 'given away', almost spitting the words out in judgement.

I will give particular weight to negative words like 'died' 'cried' and 'slain'.

The opening speech is a series of questions, so the pitch at the end of each question might go up.

I will have a sorrowful tone on 'My own dear sons', as if channelling Mrs Johnstone's thoughts.

2 This is only one interpretation of how the Narrator could be presented. Experiment with performing the same speech in the following ways:
* An ordinary Liverpudlian sharing gossip on the street.
* A figure representing the idea of 'Fate' in a tragedy
* A politician on television describing local social problems.

Use of posture, body language, gestures and expressions

How a performer stands, moves and gestures will convey information and messages to the audience.

Task B35

Look at the *Blood Brothers* production photographs below and then write three sentences describing each character's physicality. Consider:

- **Posture**: Upright or slumped? Straight or at an angle? Weight evenly balanced or off balance? Head up or down? Facing the audience, another character or looking away?
- **Stance or seated position**: Legs straight or bent? Legs close together or apart? One leg in front of the other?
- **Gestures**: Arms at the sides? Pointing? Outstretched?
- Proximity: Close to another character or distant from them? Touching another character?
- **Facial expressions**: Eyes wide open or closed? Smiling or sad? Relaxed or tense? Frowning?

> ### KEY TERM
>
> Proximity: How near people or objects are to each other; also referred to as 'proxemics', which describes the relative positions of characters on stage.

The Narrator

The Dole-ites

Mickey and Eddie

Task B36

Draw sketches showing your ideas for the posture, body language, gestures and expressions for the following moments in the play:

- Mrs Lyons on page 22 when she tells Mrs Johnstone, 'No. You'll tell nobody.'
- Mrs Johnstone on page 51, to Edward, 'God help the girls when you start dancing.'
- Mickey on page 92 when he tells Edward, 'No. I don't want your money, stuffit.'

Task B37

1 Experiment with performing the following line in a number of different ways.

> Why don't you sit down?

Perform this as if you:

- are frightened and want to calm the other person
- are commanding the other person
- love and care for the other person
- want to get away from the other person
- are busy and thinking about something else
- are playing a practical joke on the other person and will remove the chair when they try to sit.

2 How did your understanding of motivations affect your physical and vocal choices? Did you...?

- Speak more loudly or softly
- Talk more quickly or hesitantly
- Help the person into the chair or point to where the chair was
- Stress a certain word
- Move closer or farther away as you spoke
- Make or avoid eye contact.

Experimenting with vocal and physical skills

As a performer, the choices you make for using vocal and physical skills will depend on what your character is feeling and thinking, as well as the effects you want to convey to the audience.

Task B38

1 Look closely at the scene between Edward and his teacher in Act 2 (pages 65–66) and consider how the performer playing the teacher could use their vocal and physical skills to convey that he:

- is highly educated
- is powerful and used to getting his way
- dominates his students
- is used to projecting his opinions to groups of students
- has strict ideas about how boys should behave
- reacts with shock if a student speaks back to him.

2 After experimenting with the scene, write a paragraph explaining how the performer playing the teacher could use their acting skills, including:

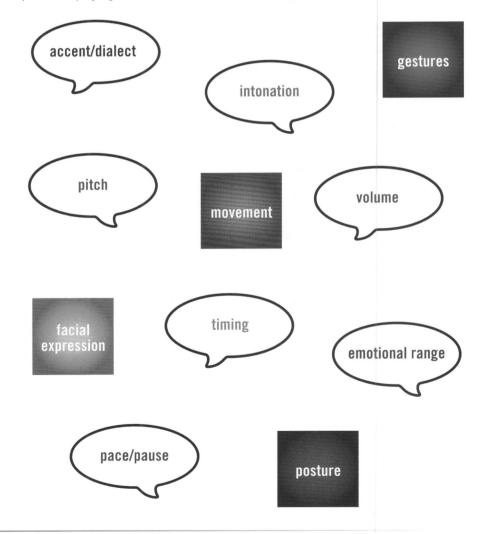

accent/dialect

gestures

intonation

pitch

movement

volume

facial expression

timing

emotional range

pace/pause

posture

Task B39

Read the following description of how a performer playing Mickey's teacher (pages 66–67) might play the role. Put a **V** next to each vocal skill described and a **P** next to each physical skill. Alternatively, use different-coloured highlighters to show vocal and physical skills.

> As Mickey's teacher, I would use a Lancashire accent, which would suggest the teacher was from near Liverpool, but at a distance that separates him from the students. My delivery would be a dull **monotone** as I go on about the Amazon Basin, showing why the students don't listen to me more. I would hunch my shoulders and read from a thick book. When I ask questions, I will suddenly look up and point at a child. My voice will get progressively louder and higher as the scene goes on, showing how rattled I am by Mickey's defiance. I will suddenly slam the book down on a desk and glare at Mickey. I will point towards the door, my arm quivering with anger when I shout, 'Out!'

Task B40

Match the character and appropriate scene with the following physical skills. (There might be more than one suitable answer.) Who might...?

- Have a slow shuffling gait   *Mickey after he gets out of prison.*
- Have a lively, bouncy walk
- Lunge with sudden violence
- Avoid making eye contact
- Have an open pleasant smile
- Have a professional, upright stance
- Shake a fist in anger
- Open eyes wide in shock
- Run frantically, panting heavily
- Wring hands anxiously
- Sit comfortably in an armchair, with a glass of whisky in hand.

KEY TERM

Monotone: A voice that doesn't change in pitch, pace or expression.

Revealing characterisation through vocal effects on dialogue

Task B41

Now you have tried out a range of vocal acting techniques, choose some that you could use on the lines in the table on page 54 to express the character and their situation.

Try to include two examples of vocal skills for each line. Think about:

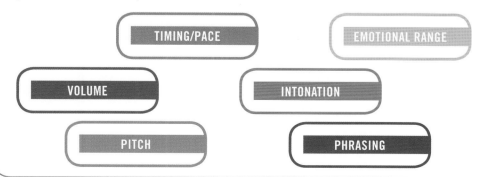

TIMING/PACE　　EMOTIONAL RANGE

VOLUME　　INTONATION

PITCH　　PHRASING

Line	Vocal skills	Details and explanation of what these choices will express to the audience
Mrs Johnstone: Nothing! Nothing. (*Pause.*) You bought me off once before…	Volume	I would shout the word 'Nothing' and then say it more quietly but emphatically, in order to make it clear that Mrs Lyons can't change my mind.
	Intonation/emotional range	I will use a bitter, angry tone, emphasising the words 'you' and 'bought' so the audience knows that I regret having given up Edward and resent Mrs Lyons' actions.
Mrs Lyons: It's your work. Your work has deteriorated.		
Linda: Take no notice, Mickey. I love you.		
Narrator: How they were born, and they died, on the selfsame day.		

Revealing characterisation through physical effects on dialogue

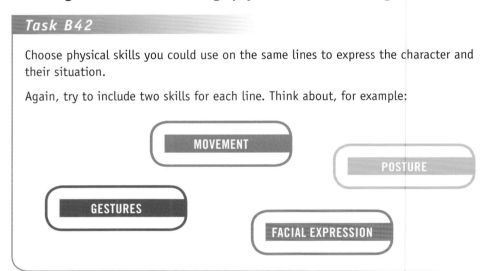

Task B42

Choose physical skills you could use on the same lines to express the character and their situation.

Again, try to include two skills for each line. Think about, for example:

MOVEMENT

POSTURE

GESTURES

FACIAL EXPRESSION

Line	Physical skills	Details and explanation of what these choices will express to the audience
Mrs Johnstone: Nothing'! Nothing. (*Pause.*) You bought me off once before…		
Mrs Lyons: It's your work. Your work has deteriorated.		
Linda: Take no notice, Mickey, I love you.	Posture	Linda will be sitting in her chair, but leaning close to Mickey. She is using her posture both to defend Mickey and as an excuse to be close to him. She will throw an arm around his neck when she says his name.
	Facial expression	At the end of the line, she will give him a pouting look, as if inviting him to kiss her.
Narrator: How they were born and they died, on the selfsame day.		

Exam-style example question: Component 1, Section B, Question 2

Task B43

1 Make plans for a response to each of the exam-style questions on the left.
2 Then choose three questions to answer in full.
Make sure that you write about both physical and vocal skills and what impact your choices will have on how the audience understands the character.

A You are performing the role of Mrs Lyons.

Describe how you would use your vocal and physical skills to perform the line below, and explain the effects you want to achieve.

'Mrs Lyons: Oh no, you're not. Edward is my son. Mine.' (page 22) [8 marks]

B You are performing the role of Mrs Johnstone.

Describe how you would use your vocal and physical skills to perform the line below, and explain the effects you want to achieve.

'Mrs Johnstone: I'll tell someone... I'll tell the police… I'll bring the police in an'…' (page 22)   [8 marks]

C You are performing the role of Mr Lyons.

Describe how you would use your vocal and physical skills to perform the line below, and explain the effects you want to achieve.

'Mr Lyons: Darling, don't be hard on the woman. She only wanted to hold the baby. All women like to hold babies, don't they?' (page 20)
                                                                                    [8 marks]

D You are performing the role of Linda.

Describe how you would use your vocal and physical skills to perform the line below, and explain the effects you want to achieve.

'Linda: Tch... you didn't tell me it was gonna be over a load of fields.' (page 70)   [8 marks]

E You are performing the role of Mickey.

Describe how you would use your vocal and physical skills to perform the line below, and explain the effects you want to achieve.

'Mickey: Why? I need... I need to take them.' (page 97)   [8 marks]

TIP

Imagine yourself fully as a performer in the named role. Whenever possible, write in the first person, for example 'I would use my voice to…'

LOOK HERE

Go to page 129 to find more information on how to write a plan for an exam response.

Sample answer: Component 1, Section B, Question 2

You are performing the role of Edward.

Describe how you would use your vocal and physical skills to perform the line below, and explain the effects you want to achieve.

'Edward: You might as well know, if I'm not going to see you again. I've always loved you, you must have known that.' (page 93) [8 marks]

Edward has returned from university and is hurt both by his fight with Mickey and by Linda who hasn't got in touch with him. He decides this is one last opportunity to tell Linda how he feels; something which, up to this point, he has avoided out of loyalty to Mickey. ①

As Edward, I would speak received pronunciation, which sounds 'posh' compared with the strong Liverpudlian dialect and accent of Linda and Mickey. ②

At university, I have gained greater confidence, which will be apparent in the more mature way I stand and hold myself, suggesting I am more a young man than a teenager. My stance would be straight and strong, shoulders back. ③

I would, however, speak hesitantly at first, pausing before I begin the line. ④ I would look searchingly into Linda's face, hoping for a chance that she returned my love. ⑤ I would let my emotions show on the phrase, 'never see you again', sounding hurt and despairing. ⑥ I would stand close to her and say the words, 'loved you' softly and tenderly. ⑦ At the end of the line, I would gently take Linda's hand. ⑧ I want the effect to be a romantic one. ⑨

I don't know that Mickey and Linda are married, so I don't realise, though the audience does, what Linda's likely response will be.

① Shows understanding of character and scene.

② Considers the vocal skill accent.

③ Uses the physical skill posture.

④ Involves the vocal skill of pacing and pauses.

⑤ Uses the physical skill eye contact.

⑥ Takes into account the vocal skills of phrasing and tone.

⑦ Considers the vocal skill tone.

⑧ Considers the physical skill gesture.

⑨ Explains the hoped-for effect on the audience.

TIP

When writing about how an actor might use physical and vocal skills, think about the effects that you might want to achieve, such as:

- An aspect of the character's background (social class, education, age, occupation)

- A character's emotional state (angry, sad, happy, in love, grief-stricken)

- Having an effect on another character (to dominate, woo, delay, amuse, pacify).

Use of performance space and interaction with other characters

You might be asked how an actor could use the performance space and interaction with other characters in relation to a specific extract from the play. You will need to show that you understand how the characters' movements, actions, reactions and interactions contribute to an audience's understanding of the play. Involved in this will be consideration of the particular effects, such as tension, comedy or romance, which the performers might try to achieve.

Read the robbery scene on pages 95–96, from the Narrator's entrance to his line, 'There's a man lies bleeding on a garage floor.' Then complete the following task.

Task B44

1 The diagram below shows an end on staging configuration and a scaffold which serves multiple purposes. On the diagram, draw and label where you would position the actors to achieve the following effects:
   • The Narrator is powerful and watching over the action.
   • Mickey is nervous and ready to distance himself from Sammy.
   • Sammy can only be partially seen, so the audience has to imagine the murder.

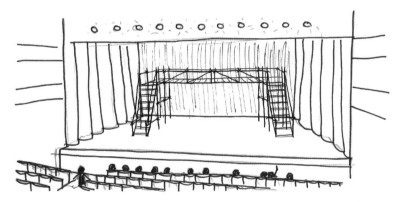

2 Looking closely at Sammy's speech in this scene, what movements and actions could be used to create tension? Consider:
   • How is Sammy moving? Smoothly or erratically? Confidently or uncertainly?
   • Does the pace of movement change? Does Sammy speed up, hesitate or slow down?
   • Are there any movements or gestures Sammy could make to attempt to frighten the unseen filling-station worker?
   • How close is Mickey to Sammy? Does he move away or closer at any point?
   • At the moment the alarm goes off, how do Sammy and Mickey react? What are their facial expressions, gestures and movements?

3 Use arrows on the diagram to show where you would have the characters move after the shooting to show:
   • Sammy wants to escape and tries to hurry Mickey.
   • The audience can see how upset Mickey is.
   • The Narrator becomes part of the scene in order to make it clear that someone has been shot.

 TIP

When writing about what you want to achieve through performance, production and staging, effects to consider could include:

   • comedy
   • tragedy
   • tension
   • romance
   • surprise
   • terror
   • sympathy
   • pity
   • alarm
   • anticipation.

Useful vocabulary for use of stage space and interaction with other characters

When writing about how space on the stage is used, you might find that some of the words and phrases detailed here will be helpful.

Proximity

How close or far away are the characters? A character might **move closer** to another character for many reasons, including because they:

▶ Are attracted to them
▶ Want to share a secret
▶ Have few personal boundaries
▶ Want to intimidate them.

Some reasons why a character might **move away** from another character are because they:

▶ Are frightened of them
▶ Want to keep something secret from them
▶ Need to be somewhere else
▶ Want to avoid facing them.

Levels

Are characters **standing** or **sitting** on the **same level**, or is **one above the other**? The positioning of characters on different levels might involve:

▶ A **high level** to show dominance or observation
▶ A **low level** to show defeat or exhaustion
▶ Sitting down to show that a character feels comfortable or at home somewhere
▶ Standing to show respect or because their job requires it
▶ Showing a character's age or social position (younger characters might be more used to sitting on the ground than older ones).

Touch

A significant type of **character interaction** is **touch**, which can show anything from love to hate. Some examples include:

▶ **Embracing** to show affection or love
▶ **Pushing** or **shoving** to demonstrate dominance or to express anger
▶ Assisting another character by **guiding** them or **handing** them objects
▶ Being **in contact** because an activity requires it, such as dancing.

Stage positions

In order to describe the characters **movements**, such as entrances, exits, **crosses** and taking centre stage, it is useful to use the correct terms for stage **positions**. For example:

▶ A character might move **centre stage** or **downstage** in order to attract attention or connect with the audience.

▶ Characters might make **counter-crosses**, such as one moving **downstage right**, while another moves **upstage left**, in order to avoid each other.

▶ Characters might enter **upstage** so they face the audience as they come on or they might enter **downstage**, with their backs to the audience.

KEY TERMS

Crosses: Movements from one section of the stage to another.

Counter-crosses: Movement in opposition to another character's cross, so, one going stage left when the other goes stage right. This might be to balance the stage picture or to demonstrate an aspect of the characters' relationship.

Pace and style of movement

In order to create specific effects, consider the **speed** at which movements might be done and in what **style**, for example:

▶ **Slowly,** including use of slow motion, to emphasise a moment or to create tension

▶ **Quickly,** such as fast **exaggerated** movements for comedy

▶ Slow, **graceful**, **fluid** movements to create a dreamy or romantic effect

▶ Quick, **violent** movements to demonstrate anger or force.

Reactions

Movements or **actions** triggered by something that happens include:

▶ Something another character says or does

▶ A sound, like a gunshot or telephone call, or a lighting effect suggesting rain or night-time

▶ The entrances or exits of other characters.

 TIP

Precise details are vital for achieving top marks. Avoid vague, general comments.

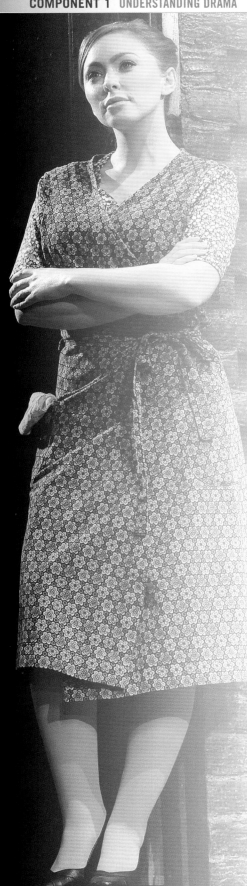

Characters' movements in *Blood Brothers*

Task B45

Use your knowledge of the play to consider character movements. Find at least one instance when the following character movements and actions could take place:

- A character embraces another.   *Mrs Johnstone hugs Edward when he cries about moving away from Mickey.*
- One character kisses another.
- Two characters dance.
- Three characters pose for a photograph.
- One character attacks another.
- Two characters sit at the same level.
- Three characters stand at the same level.
- One character sits while another stands.

Task B46

1 Look closely at the scene between Edward and Mrs Johnstone on page 50, from 'What's up?' to 'We're a right pair, aren't we?'

   Imagine you are playing Mrs Johnstone. Make notes on the following aspects of staging and performance. Use the vocabulary notes on pages 60–61 of this book to help you.

   - **Proximity:** How close will you be to Edward? Will this change during the scene?
   - **Levels:** Will you be standing or seated? Will this change during the scene?
   - **Touch:** How will you perform the stage direction 'cradles him'. Are you sitting down or standing up? Do you put your arms around him? Does he rest his head on you?
   - **Stage positions:** Where on the stage are you? How does this position affect the audience's understanding of the extract?
   - **Pace and style of movement:** Do you move quickly or slowly? Do you pause or change tempo? Do you treat Edward gently or roughly?
   - **Reactions:** Do you move because of something Edward does? In reaction to him, do you make certain gestures or change your facial expressions and body language?

2 Continue to imagine you are performing the role of Mrs Johnstone. Again, focus on the extract specified above.

   Explain how you and the actor playing Edward might use the performance space and interact with each other to create sympathy for the characters.

Exam-style example questions: Component 1, Section B, Question 3

A Focus on pages 36–37 of the script, from 'Edward: Well. Well it's true' to 'Mrs Lyons: Oh my son…'

You are performing the role of Mrs Lyons.

Explain how you and the actor playing Edward might use the performance space and interact with each other to **create tension** for your audience.

[12 marks]

B Focus on page 47 of the script, from the entrance of the Policeman to the three children beginning to cry.

You are performing the role of Edward.

Explain how you and the actors playing Linda, Mickey and the Policeman might use the performance space and interact with each other to **create comedy** for your audience.

[12 marks]

C Focus on page 71 of the script, from 'Mickey: There's that lad…' to Linda's exit.

You are performing the role of Linda.

Explain how you and the actor playing Mickey might use the performance space and interact with each other to **relay the feelings the characters have for each other** to your audience.

[12 marks]

D Focus on page 73 of the script, from 'Edward: Hi.' to 'Edward: 'My God I only live…'

You are performing the role of Mickey.

Explain how you and the actor playing Edward might use the performance space and interact with each other to **show contrasts between the characters** to your audience.

[12 marks]

E Focus on pages 77–78 of the script, from 'Mrs Lyons: Are you always going to follow me?' to 'Mrs Johnstone: He is yours.'

You are performing the role of Mrs Lyons.

Explain how you and the actor playing Mrs Johnstone might use the performance space and interact with each other to **emphasise the conflict between the characters** for your audience.

[12 marks]

Task B47

Write a plan for each of the exam-style questions on this page. Remember to include:

- The location of the scene (Mrs Johnstone's kitchen, the school, the field and so on) and how that might influence your movements
- How movements and interactions create the effects that the question has asked for (tension, comedy, romance, insight into the characters or their relationships, conflict…)
- Where the scene might be positioned (Using the whole stage? Downstage? An upper platform?)
- When and why your characters might move
- Gestures they might make and body language they use
- How the characters react physically to each other.

 TIP

The best answers are well developed and note precise details, including any changes in emotions, mood or relationships.

Sample answer: Component 1, Section B, Question 3

① Explains context of scene, demonstrating understanding of the play.

② Shows understanding of play and how sympathy could be created.

③ Precise details of how performance space could be used.

④ Details of how use of space could be developed.

⑤ Interaction with Mickey (proximity/touch).

⑥ Interaction with Mickey (physical reactions).

⑦ Details of how desired effect could be created through performances.

⑧ Explanation of motivations and effect on audience.

Task B48

1 Make a plan for a paragraph you could add to complete this response, which covers:
   - Use of stage space, including the furniture in the kitchen, levels and positioning on stage
   - Interaction with Mickey when he is describing the games he played
   - The impression that the audience will have of Mrs Johnstone at the end of this extract.

Focus on page 24, from 'Mickey aged seven is knocking…' to 'Mrs Johnstone: Good.'

You are playing Mrs Johnstone.

Explain how you and the actor playing Mickey might use the performance space and interact with each other to create **sympathy for the characters**.

[12 marks]

Right before this scene, the audience has seen Mrs Johnstone give away Edward. The Narrator reminds Mrs Johnstone of her superstitions and she is frightened and upset. ①

In this extract, the audience can see that Mrs Johnstone is trying to do her best for her children, including Mickey who is now seven, which should make the audience more sympathetic to her. ②

As Mrs Johnstone, I would establish that the kitchen is the centre of my life and when I am inside it, I feel no one can get to me. In my imagination, the banging at the door makes me think I am in trouble (the Narrator's song suggests the devil is going to get me), so I would lean against the kitchen door, place my hands over my ears to block out the noise, close my eyes tightly and shout, 'Go away.' ③ However, once I hear my son's voice, I would snap out of my anxious thoughts and open my eyes. I would sag against the door in relief and my face would relax. ④

I would quickly pull Mickey in and, standing in the centre of the kitchen, hug him tightly against me. ⑤ Little boys often don't like hugs, so the actor playing Mickey would probably squirm in my arms, pulling annoyed faces, but I would keep a firm hold on him. ⑥ He might half turn away from me and face downstage, so the audience can see our contrasting expressions. While he looks embarrassed, my expression would show my happiness and relief, realising I'd been silly to worry. ⑦ Our close proximity would create sympathy for Mrs Johnstone as the audience will be able to see how much she loves Mickey and how she is tortured by her decision to give Edward away. ⑧

Interpretations of characters

The performers and creative team interpret a play, making choices about what features to emphasise in the play and its characters in order to express their understanding of and ideas about the play's meanings, moods and styles.

Task B49

Read the following interpretations of characters, that have been written from the character's perspective. Identify which character's feelings, thoughts and motivations are being expressed. In addition, try to recall scenes or lines of dialogue that might have led to these interpretations.

> I'm someone who always tries to look on the bright side. If I dwelt on my problems, I'd never get out of bed! I've got my hands full, having so many children and none of them angels, but I think I've managed pretty well. Sometimes I think back to the day when I made that bargain, but it's no use crying over spilt milk.

> My job takes up most of my time. I have a matter-of-fact, business-like way of taking care of tasks, even unpleasant ones like firing people. I have a mild, educated voice and, when at work, show no emotion at all. At home, however, my wife sometimes annoys and worries me and I can snap at her when aggravated. But mainly, I try to keep the peace.

> I serve as Mrs Johnstone's conscience and remind her of her terrible deed. I often stand closely behind her, as if whispering in her ear. I sometimes assist her, handing her a coat, for example, as if I am controlling her actions and the progress of the play.

> I've been lucky in so many ways, but there was an emptiness in my life because my husband and I couldn't have children. I hid my pain, occupying myself with shopping and making sure my husband came back to a lovely, calm home. Once there was a chance of having a child, however, I became obsessed. I'm not sure I ever had a moment's peace after that fateful exchange.

> I adore Mickey and will do anything to get his attention. In school, I lean forward as if trying to kiss him and, later, I embarrass him when he tries to help me.

> I don't want to work at conventional jobs and am always looking for a shortcut. I have a powerful personality, so can often get my way by threatening and bullying others, sometimes by pushing them around or shouting at them. I hold my head high and don't try to pretend to be anything other than what I am.

 TIP

Among the choices you might make in your interpretation is how naturalistic or stylised the performances and design will be.

Interpreting the Narrator

There is less biographical information about the Narrator than most of the other characters in the play. He is used differently from the 'realistic' characters. As so little is known about him – even his name remains a mystery – you might feel this gives you more freedom in how his character could be interpreted.

Task B50

Below are three different interpretations of the Narrator's costume and performance. Read them and decide which one you feel best expresses your understanding of the character and play.

Which interpretation do you prefer, and why?

What is your own interpretation?

In my interpretation of the Narrator, he represents the unfairness of social class in Liverpool. I dress him in a workman's navy overalls, and, poking out from his pocket he has a P45 form, which employees are given when they are fired. In the 'Take a Letter Miss Jones' scene he would join the 'Dole-ites', who would be dressed identically to him. He would have a harsh tone of voice and use sharp, jabbing gestures.

As the Narrator, I would be dressed as a rock star, like Noddy Holder from the group Slade, who, although they were from Wolverhampton rather than Liverpool, were distinctive and popular in the 1970s. He would represent youth and music which were important in Liverpool. I would wear a colourful plaid waistcoat, bell-bottom trousers and a top hat. I would bounce and prowl around the stage and, at times, walk into the audience to observe the action. My cheery tone of voice would darken as the play heads towards its tragic conclusion.

TIP

There is no one 'right' interpretation of a character. Your interpretation of a character should be based on your understanding of the character's background, motivations and importance to the play.

I think of the Narrator as an angel of death. From the beginning of the play, he is talking about death and reminds the audience that events are going to take a negative turn. Therefore, I would dress him entirely in black, including a black turtleneck or shirt and a long black coat. He would usually be standing very still, sometimes high on the scaffolding, looking down on the action. Sometimes he will move his arms in a sweeping gesture as if he is conducting the action, such as bringing in new characters. His voice will be calm and well-modulated, with just a hint of a Liverpool accent.

Exploring acting skills based on an extract from the play

For your final question in Section B of Component 1, you will have a choice to write about either a performance or design skill. If you choose to write about performance, you will need to discuss the acting skills necessary for a performer playing the character named in the question for both the given extract and the rest of the play.

Showing understanding of the play, the characters and performance skills

Before you can consider exactly what acting skills are necessary for performing a particular character, you need to ensure that you understand the character, including:

▸ Their importance in the play
▸ Their relationships with other characters
▸ The context/s in which they are seen.

You will also need to develop your own interpretation of the character, based on your understanding of the play. This means that there is no one 'right' answer for this question. Make sure, however, that you do not contradict the facts of the play. You should be confident, for example, of how the actors will use their skills to show their age, social class, emotional state and motivations as appropriate for the play.

You can build on your understanding of physical and vocal skills, as well as use of performance space and interaction with others. This question, however, also requires a wider understanding of the play and how characters might change during the course of the play.

Task B51

Use a grid like this to make notes on key characters at three points in the play.

Character	First key moment	Second key moment	Third key moment
Mrs Johnstone	First scene with Mrs Lyons	When Mrs Lyons attacks her	At the end of the play, when Mickey confronts Edward
Interpretation	She is an open, warm character, who is struggling to get by. She tries to make the best of a bad situation.		
Important line	'It's such a lovely house it's a pleasure to clean it.'		
Physical skills	She is respectful to Mrs Lyons and wouldn't sit in her presence. She keeps working while she is speaking to her.		
Vocal skills	Strong Liverpool accent, warm, friendly tones.		

Table continued on next page ▸

Task B52

Consider the character of Mickey and make notes on the following six points, including vocal and physical skills.

1 Who Mickey is and why he is important in the play.
2 The style and context of the play and how those might affect the actor's choices.
3 First impressions of Mickey at age seven.
4 How Mickey changes by age 14.
5 How Mickey changes at 18.
6 How Mickey changes when he gets out of prison.

Table continued from previous page ▶

Character	First key moment	Second key moment	Third key moment
Mrs Lyons	When she convinces Mrs Johnstone to give up her baby	When she wants to move away	The attack on Mrs Johnstone
Interpretation			
Important line			
Physical skills			
Vocal skills			
Mickey	When he first meets Edward	On the field with Linda	Arguing with Linda over the pills
Interpretation			
Important line			
Physical skills			
Vocal skills			
Edward	When he first meets Mickey	As a teenager, reunited with Mickey	Telling Linda how he feels about her
Interpretation			
Important line			
Physical skills			
Vocal skills			
Linda	Defending Mickey from Sammy	Sticking up for Mickey at school	Trying to get Mickey to stop taking pills
Interpretation			
Important line			
Physical skills			
Vocal skills			
Sammy	Trying to bully seven-year-old Mickey	When he robs the bus conductor	When he convinces Mickey to take part in the robbery
Interpretation			
Important line			
Physical skills			
Vocal skills			
Mr Lyons	When he doesn't want Mrs Lyons to fire Mrs Johnstone	Losing his temper at Mrs Lyons for worrying about Edward	When he fires the employees
Interpretation			
Important line			
Physical skills			
Vocal skills			

Extending acting skills from an extract to the rest of the play

Task B53

Read the airgun scene from Act 1 (from 'Linda: Missed!' to the entrance of the Policeman) and then write an answer for the following exam-style question:

> You are performing the role of Linda.
> Describe how you would use your acting skills to interpret Linda's character in this extract and explain why your ideas are appropriate both for this extract and the play as a whole.

 TIP

Remember to select specific lines, stage directions or moments from the play to support your ideas.

You might use a plan similar to this one:

1. Linda's importance in the play, as the love interest for the two boys.

2. The Liverpool setting and expectations of girls at this time. How Linda's skill at shooting might be surprising.

3. How the actor playing Linda uses her vocal and physical skills to indicate her age, background and personality.

4. When she might use the stage space and interaction with the two boys to create comedy.

5. Contrast this scene with impressions of Linda as a teenager and how she has changed.

6. Contrast this scene with Linda when she is in her 20s and looking after Mickey.

7. Conclusion: How Linda's role changes in the play from a comic one to a tragic one.

 TIP

In the exam, you can answer either Question 4 (performance) or Question 5 (design). Whichever you choose, it will be worth the most marks in Section B, so your answer needs to be well-developed, using precise details from the extract and examples of how the character could be performed in the rest of the play.

How to create a plan for Section B, Question 4

Remember that, when planning your response for Question 4, you should make sure that you write about both the given extract and the play as a whole. Below is a suggested plan in response to the following Question 4 example:

KEY TERM

Adrenaline: A hormone that produces heightened energy and excitement when facing dangerous, frightening or competitive situations.

Focus on pages 95–96, from Sammy's entrance to the arrival of the Policemen. You are performing the role of Sammy.

Describe how you would use your acting skills to interpret Sammy's character in this extract and explain why your ideas are appropriate both for this extract and the play as a whole.

Plan

1 Sammy's importance in the play and how he is perceived by the other characters and the audience.

2 Extract:
- What Sammy wants in this scene: to get money.
- What he does to get what he wants: threatens and kills filling-station worker.
- My interpretation: He is running high on adrenaline and out of control. He expects the worker to just hand over money, like others have done in the past, and can't believe it when he hits the alarm instead.

- **Vocal skills:**
  - Strong Liverpool accent
  - Tone: Harsh, aggressive. Emphasises words like 'piss'
  - Volume: Raises voice on 'Y' don't get up' to increase threat
  - Pace: Goes more quickly when he realises the worker is going to hit alarm button
  - Tone/Pace: Panicked on 'Quick'
  - Tone: Sarcastic on 'I know I bloody did'
  - Pitch: Low bass tones, but gets higher when nervous.

- **Physical skills:**
  - Posture: Leans forward aggressively
  - Gestures: Suddenly lashes out
  - Facial expression: Furrows brow in anger at worker;
  - Gestures: Shakes gun in worker's face
  - Facial expression: Eyes open wide in shock at shooting
  - Movement: In slow motion, reacts to gunshot
  - Interaction: Pushes Mickey on the word 'Move'.

3 Rest of play:

- Sammy at 'nearly ten': Dominates the other children, although Linda gets the better of him in their confrontation.

  – Vocal skills: Voice lighter than in extract, but strong accent and aggressive tone already obvious.

  – Physical skills: Tries to act older than he is, towers over other children and makes aggressive gestures like pointing and shoving. Tries to maintain high status even when retreating from Linda, by holding his head high and signalling to others to follow him.

- Sammy at 16: More seriously threatening than when a child. Acts innocently at first when he tries to underpay on the bus, but quickly becomes threatening.

  – Vocal: Changes from a calm tone on 'same for me' to furious and shocking on 'shut it.' Barks out commands and threats.

  – Physical: Moves quickly, threatens conductor with a knife, jumps off bus, runs to escape.

4 Conclusion:

Sammy's development through the play shows how the seeds of his disturbed, violent personality grow into his later criminal behaviour. His reckless fearlessness lands both Mickey and him in prison.

Task B54

Use the template given here to create your own plan for one of the exam-style questions that follow:

1 Character's importance in play. How they are perceived by other characters and the audience:

2 What the character wants in this extract:

3 What the character is doing to get what they want:

4 Your interpretation of the character:

5 Extract:
  – Vocal skills
  – Physical skills

6 Rest of play:
  – Vocal skills
  – Physical skills

7 Conclusion:

TIP

In an exam, you will not be able to write a plan as detailed as this, but it is a good form of revision, so that you get into the habit of shaping your answers and covering all the necessary points.

LOOK HERE

For more examples and advice on creating plans for exam answers, go to page 129.

Exam-style example questions: Component 1, Section B, Question 4

A Focus on page 49, from Edward's 'Why Daddy?' to 'But I'd much rather live here.'

You are performing the role of Edward.

Describe how you would use your acting skills to interpret Edward's character in this extract, and explain why your ideas are appropriate both for this extract and the play as a whole. [20 marks]

B Focus on pages 63–64, from 'Sammy: Same for me' to 'Sammy: No mark!'

You are performing the role of Sammy.

Describe how you would use your acting skills to interpret Sammy's character in this extract, and explain why your ideas are appropriate both for this extract and the play as a whole. [20 marks]

C Focus on pages 44–45, from Mr Lyons' entrance to 'Mr Lyons: Oh Christ.'

You are performing the role of Mr Lyons.

Describe how you would use your acting skills to interpret Mr Lyons' character in this extract, and explain why your ideas are appropriate both for this extract and the play as a whole. [20 marks]

D Focus on page 22, from 'Mrs Johnstone: Left where?' to 'Mrs Johnstone (*terrified*): What? What?'.

You are performing the role of Mrs Johnstone.

Describe how you would use your acting skills to interpret Mrs Johnstone's character in this extract, and explain why your ideas are appropriate both for this extract and the play as a whole. [20 marks]

 TIP

Early in your revision, you might want to answer questions like this without timing your writing so that you can answer as fully as possible. As the exam date nears, however, it is a good idea to practise using correct timings.

 **LOOK HERE**

The notes on page 133 offer more ideas on how to use your time wisely in the exam.

Sample answer: Component 1, Section B, Question 4

Study this extract from a candidate-style answer about the character of Linda on page 41 and the rest of the play.

Throughout the play, Linda is portrayed as a strong, loving person who tries to make the best of whatever situation she is in. In this extract, we see Linda, at age seven, when she is shown to be an assertive, confident girl with a great loyalty to Mickey. In this excerpt, she stands up to Sammy who is bullying Mickey. ① In order to show her fearlessness, I would stand with my legs planted far apart and my hands on my hips. ② I will hold Sammy's gaze when I say 'you'll all go to hell,' emphasising the word 'hell' as it will seem like a very shocking word for me to say – probably one I have heard but possibly never said aloud before. ③ My accent will be a working class Liverpool dialect and my voice will be somewhat higher pitched to show my youthfulness. ④ My whole attitude will show that I am comfortable playing on the streets and not afraid of talking to older children, like Sammy. ⑤ I will use the stage space to show my protectiveness of Mickey, by standing between Mickey and the other children and putting my arm around him, keeping a close proximity to him. ⑥ When I threaten to tell my mother about Sammy's stealing her cigarettes, I will slowly approach him and point my finger in his face. ⑦ This gesture will seem very daring and rather comic as I am the only one not frightened of Sammy. ⑧

① Demonstrates understanding of excerpt and character.

② Describes physical skills (posture).

③ In detail, describes physical skill (eye contact) and vocal skill (emphasis), justifies choices.

④ Describes vocal skills using correct terminology.

⑤ Justifies and analyses effect of choices.

⑥ Describes use of stage space and interaction.

⑦ Precise detail, describing pace, movement and gesture.

⑧ Analyses effect of gesture.

In addition to analysing the extract, you must remember to raise relevant points about how acting skills could be used in other sections of the play. The character might have developed and changed in the course of the play, so your acting choices are likely to be different, but must make sense in terms of your interpretation of the play. In the case of Linda, for example, you could write about how this protectiveness of Mickey is also shown in other scenes of the play, and also how she develops and changes as she matures.

Task B55

Use the questions on the previous page as practice examination questions or for practice in making detailed plans.

Exploring design skills based on an extract from the play

If you decide to answer Question 5 (Design) rather than Question 4 (Performance), you will need to choose one design specialism and explain how you would use it to support the action of the extract and the rest of the play.

Among the design choices you could make are:

costume   set   lighting   sound

Whichever design specialism you choose to focus on, there are several points you should consider.

TIP

Unless otherwise specified, Question 5 will not restrict you to the given context of the play (unlike Question 1). You might choose to reflect the play's actual context, or you could create a more stylised or symbolic use of design to emphasise the play's themes or moods or to make it relevant to a particular modern audience.

Task B56

Use the theatre-in-the-round staging configuration to sketch a set design for the following three moments in the play:

1 The play's opening
2 The field scene
3 The pill scene.

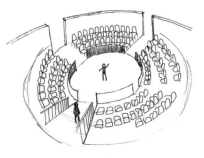

Make notes on how the set would work, for example what would be brought on for each scene (additional furniture, sets) and where characters would be positioned for key moments.

The **technical requirements** of your design

- Your design should be an achievable creation rather than an impossible wish list.
- You need to show that you have at least a basic understanding of how your design will work on stage.
- You should use the correct technical terminology in describing your design.

Your **concept**

This is your overall approach to explain how your design will enrich the production, such as drawing out the play's themes and the location and the period in which you are setting it.

Your **inspiration**

You might also want to mention what has inspired your design, such as your understanding of the context of the play, your interpretation of the play's style, or the influence of the work of other designers or artists, to show that you understand the creative process of creating theatre.

How your design is **appropriate** for the extract and the rest of the play

You need to demonstrate that you understand not only the specific demands of the extract, but other key moments in the play that would be supported by your design.

Writing about costume design

When describing your ideas for costumes, you might consider:

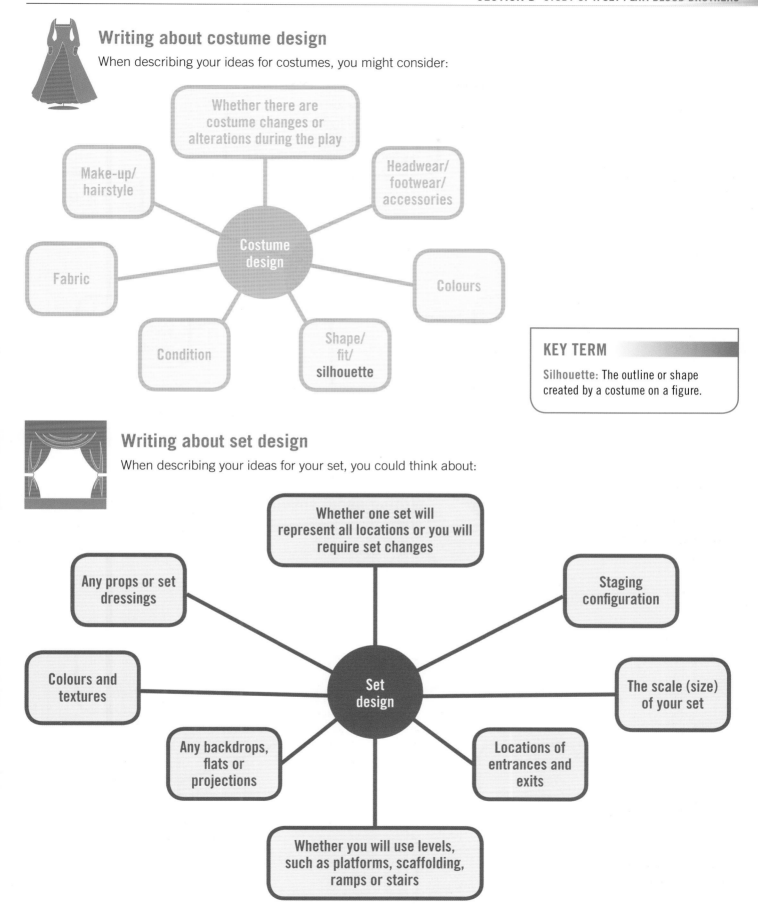

KEY TERM

Silhouette: The outline or shape created by a costume on a figure.

Writing about set design

When describing your ideas for your set, you could think about:

Writing about lighting design

When describing your ideas for lighting design, you might include:

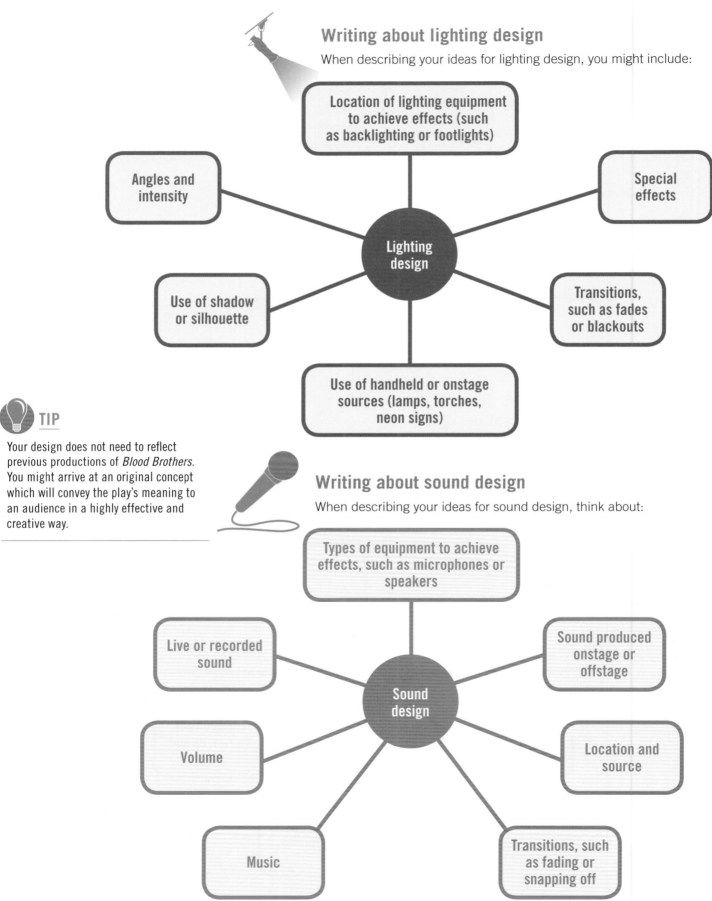

Location of lighting equipment to achieve effects (such as backlighting or footlights)

Angles and intensity

Special effects

Lighting design

Use of shadow or silhouette

Transitions, such as fades or blackouts

Use of handheld or onstage sources (lamps, torches, neon signs)

TIP

Your design does not need to reflect previous productions of *Blood Brothers*. You might arrive at an original concept which will convey the play's meaning to an audience in a highly effective and creative way.

Writing about sound design

When describing your ideas for sound design, think about:

Types of equipment to achieve effects, such as microphones or speakers

Live or recorded sound

Sound produced onstage or offstage

Sound design

Volume

Location and source

Music

Transitions, such as fading or snapping off

Design ideas for an extract and the whole play

Task B57

Read Act 2, pages 63–64, from 'The 'bus' appears...' to 'The Conductor rings the bell.'
Then complete the following grid with design ideas for each of the specialisms.

	Design ideas and suggested challenges of extract	Examples	Details in extract	Rest of play (pick key moments to discuss in detail)
Costume	Need to establish that Linda and Mickey are young teenagers going to school and Sammy is older and more dangerous.		Fabrics: Colours: Fit/condition: Footwear/accessories:	
Set	Transition from **domestic** scene to bus. Bus set needs to be quickly created for brief scene. Make sure that the action can be seen.		Staging configuration: Colours: Materials: Levels: Props:	
Lighting	Change from domestic scenes to outdoor and bus lighting. Special lighting used to create the 'bus'.		Colours: Angles/intensity: Special effects: Transitions:	
Sound	Make the transition from domestic setting to bus. Sounds used to establish bus, such as traffic noises, brakes and bell.		Volume: Live or recorded: On stage or off: Transitions:	

Task B58

1 At the end of Act 1, the characters move home and to what they hope will be a new start. Read from 'Mickey comes out of the house' on page 51 to 'He exits' on page 52. Focusing on sound, lighting or set (choose only one), write a paragraph describing how your design ideas will help to show the changes in the characters' lives and support the mood and actions of this extract.

2 Then write a second paragraph with your design ideas for the rest of the play, focusing on three different key moments to discuss in detail.

Task B59

1 Focus on page 92 of the script, and sketch contrasting costumes for Mickey and Edward.

2 Then describe how, as a costume designer, your costume design creates effects that support the action of this extract. Explain why your ideas are appropriate both for this extract and the play as a whole.

KEY TERM

Domestic: Related to activities in a home or within a family.

 **LOOK HERE**

For more ideas about costume design, go to page 99 and, for set design, page 106.

How to create a plan for Section B, Question 5

The following suggestion is a sample plan for answering Question 5 in the exam, with notes on what you need to consider and include.

TIP

You might choose to draw a quick sketch as part of your answer if that helps you to explain your ideas more clearly and efficiently.

1

Design specialism you have chosen and your approach to the play.

2

The demands of the particular extract, for example:
- time period
- time of day
- season
- location
- style
- actions
- mood.

3

How your design will be realised in the extract, for example, depending on the specialism you have chosen:
- materials or technology needed
- how transitions will be handled
- volume of sound
- intensity of lighting
- fabrics and colours of costumes.

4

How your design will be realised in the rest of the play.
- Key moment one:
- Key moment two:
- Key moment three:

5

Why your design approach is appropriate for a production of *Blood Brothers*.

Exam-style example questions: Component 1, Section B, Question 5

A Focus on pages 10 and 11, from 'Mrs Lyons enters' to 'The Narrator enters.'

You are a designer working on one aspect of design for this extract.

Describe how you would use your design skills to create effects that support the action of this extract, and explain why your ideas are appropriate both for this extract and the play as a whole. [20 marks]

B Focus on pages 47–48, from 'The Policeman goes to confront Mrs Johnstone' to 'The Policeman leaves.'

Describe how you would use your design skills to create effects that support the message and action of this extract, and explain why your ideas are appropriate both for this extract and the play as a whole. [20 marks]

C Focus on pages 82–83, from 'There's a few bob in your pocket' to 'Linda, Mickey and Edward exit.'

Describe how you would use your design skills to create effects that support the mood and actions of this extract, and explain why your ideas are appropriate both for this extract and the play as a whole. [20 marks]

Task B60

Choose one of the questions above and make a detailed plan for how you would answer it. You might find some of these sentence starters useful:

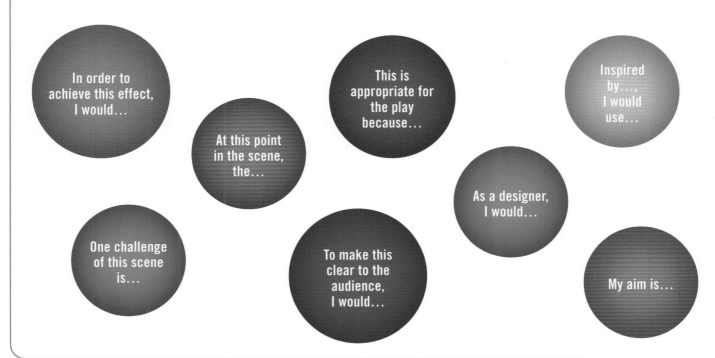

In order to achieve this effect, I would...

At this point in the scene, the...

This is appropriate for the play because...

Inspired by..., I would use...

As a designer, I would...

One challenge of this scene is...

To make this clear to the audience, I would...

My aim is...

Sample answers for Component 1, Section B, Question 5

> Focus on pages 104–105, from 'Mrs Johnstone hammers on Linda's door…' to 'Mickey: Stay where you are!'
>
> Describe how you would use your design skills to create effects that support the mood and actions of this extract and explain why your ideas are appropriate both for this extract and the play as a whole. [20 marks]

Task B61

The following three extracts are from three student-style responses to the question above. Read them and put:

- **T** next to any examples of correct terminology
- **C** next to creative ideas
- **U** next to any points which show understanding.

KEY TERMS

Fresnel: A lantern with a lens that produces a soft-edged beam of light.

Followspot: A powerful spotlight operated so that its beam follows an actor around the stage.

1   At this point, the play is approaching its climax and, as a lighting designer, I will want to increase the intensity and tension of this scene. I will use red filters in the fresnel lanterns to provide a red glowing wash across the stage in order to highlight the desperation of the Johnstones. I will use a followspot to track Mrs Johnstone as she races around the stage.

To make the Narrator seem frightening, I will use bright footlights which will cast harsh shadows on his face, as he creates the mood for the audience of the final tragic ending. He will also be spotlit, with the light narrowing to a pinpoint so it is just on his face on the final 'TODAY' which will make him seem ghostly and inhuman. Immediately after the word 'today', there will be a blackout and the lights will slowly fade up to the Town Hall, with a white wash across the stage and a yellow golden light coming diagonally down from profile spots to resemble light from a window. This will shower Edward in a pleasant light, to contrast him with Mickey and his despair.

This transition will provide a moment of calm before the violent ending to come.

2 As a set designer, I want to provide levels and ramps in order to create excitement and tension as the characters rush from location to location. I will design my set on a traverse stage.

At one end of the traverse, I will have black scaffolding, from which the Narrator will deliver his lines, while Mrs Johnstone and Linda can be seen running up the ramps to the centre stage of the traverse, then splitting in opposite directions to look for Mickey. Linda will run towards the scaffolding, while Mrs Johnstone runs towards the other end, where there is a raised wooden platform, with a table and two chairs. This will represent the Town Hall, which the actors can reach by using one of the two sets of stairs.

Edward will be seen slowly walking up the stairs stage left, as if to his death, while the Narrator repeats 'Today'.

3 Sound design has an important role to play in creating the chaos and confusion before the ending of the play. Instead of realistic sound, as sound designer, I would choose non-naturalistic, overly amplified sounds. For example, I would record the sound of Mrs Johnstone's hammering on the door and play it at a loud volume, with an added reverb, to make it more frightening. I want to capture the atmosphere of the city, so I will create a recording of city noises to underscore Mrs Johnstone and Linda's search for Mickey, as well as having sirens and alarms going off.

I want the audience to feel involved so will have positioned speakers around the back of the auditorium and on the sides, so they will feel surrounded by all the noise. At the end of the Narrator's chorus, the sound will suddenly snap off, creating an empty eerie effect, leaving the audience wondering what will happen next.

TIP

Think, 'CUT':
- Creative
- Understanding
- Terminology.

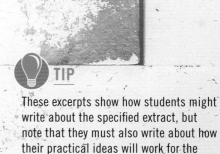

TIP

These excerpts show how students might write about the specified extract, but note that they must also write about how their practical ideas will work for the rest of the play as well.

TEST YOURSELF B6

Match the correct definition with each technical term used in theatre performance and design.

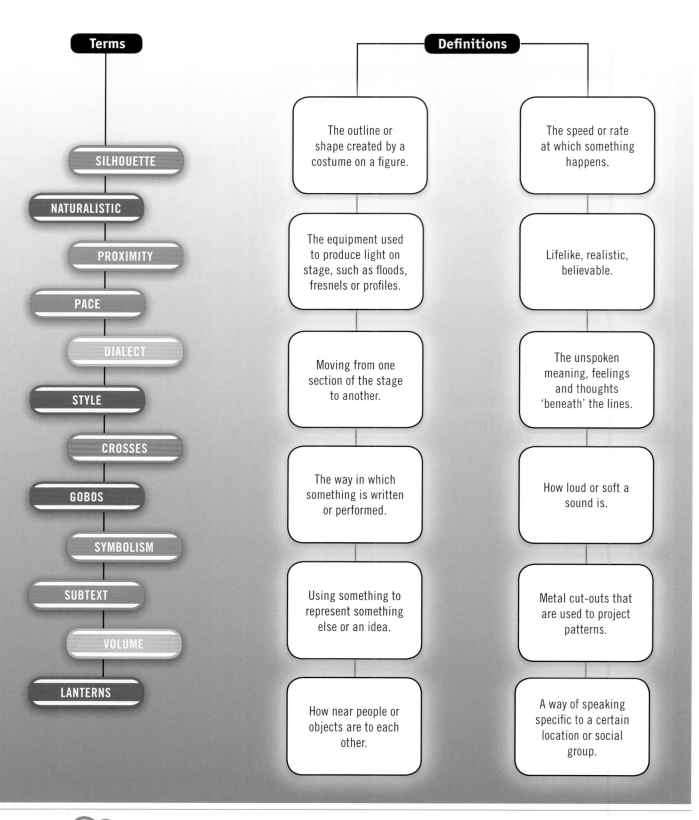

Terms	Definitions
SILHOUETTE	The outline or shape created by a costume on a figure.
NATURALISTIC	The speed or rate at which something happens.
PROXIMITY	The equipment used to produce light on stage, such as floods, fresnels or profiles.
PACE	Lifelike, realistic, believable.
DIALECT	Moving from one section of the stage to another.
STYLE	The unspoken meaning, feelings and thoughts 'beneath' the lines.
CROSSES	The way in which something is written or performed.
GOBOS	How loud or soft a sound is.
SYMBOLISM	Using something to represent something else or an idea.
SUBTEXT	Metal cut-outs that are used to project patterns.
VOLUME	How near people or objects are to each other.
LANTERNS	A way of speaking specific to a certain location or social group.

www.illuminatepublishing.com/drama

LEARNING CHECKLIST: SECTION B

Tick each aspect of your understanding of *Blood Brothers* if you are confident of your knowledge.

If you are unsure of anything, go back and revise.

Do you know…?

How to describe the use of the performance space and character interaction

The context of the play, including time period and location

How to plan an answer to an exam question about the set play

How to write about an extract and expand it to the rest of the play, including choosing key moments to discuss in detail

How to write about acting skills, including correct terminology

How the context could be reflected by costume, set, sound and lighting design

At least four physical skills actors can use

That everyone must answer the first three questions in the exam

At least four vocal skills actors can use

The names of all the characters and their importance to the plot

That you will have a choice whether to answer either Question 4 (performance) or 5 (your choice of design specialism)

How to write about design skills, including correct terminology

SECTION C

LIVE THEATRE PRODUCTION

Assessment focus:

AO3: Demonstrate knowledge and understanding of how drama and theatre is developed and performed.

AO4: Analyse and evaluate the work of others.

What the specification says...

In Section C, students answer one question (from a choice) on the work of theatre makers in a single live production.

They should be able to discuss:

▶ a variety of aspects of one production, giving a personal analysis and evaluation of the theatrical elements

▶ how successfully meaning was communicated to the audience.

TIP

The play you analyse for Section C must be different from your Section B set play. You might have seen a live production of *Blood Brothers*, but, if you are writing about *Blood Brothers* for Section B, you cannot write about it for Section C.

Noma Dumezweni in *Linda* ▶

Analysing and evaluating live theatre

For Section C of your written examination, you will need to choose one question about a theatre production you have seen. You may write about **performance skills** *or* **design skills**.

In order to prepare for this question, you will:

▶ View a live theatre production

▶ Make notes on different performance and design elements

▶ Analyse how the performers' acting and a particular designer's skills helped to communicate the characters, action and style of the play to the audience.

What are production elements?

When you see a performance of a play, you might notice its overall impact and whether or not you enjoyed it, rather than thinking about separating it into its many different elements. However, one of the requirements of a live theatre evaluation is to recognise how the different production elements contribute to the overall interpretation and success of the play. You must be able to consider how the performers and designers each helped to establish the meaning of the play.

There is a range of production elements to be explored when discussing live theatre.

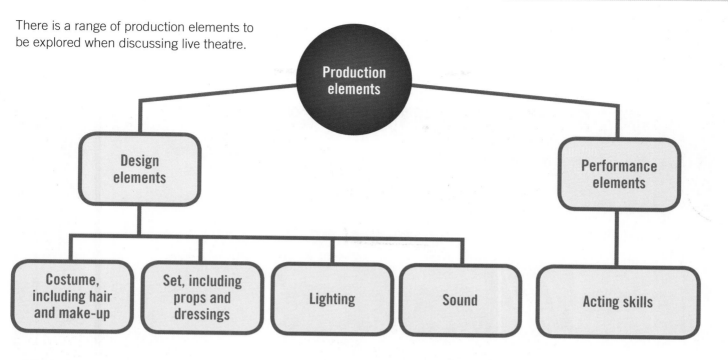

 TEST YOURSELF C1

Decide which production elements are being discussed in the following points. Select from:

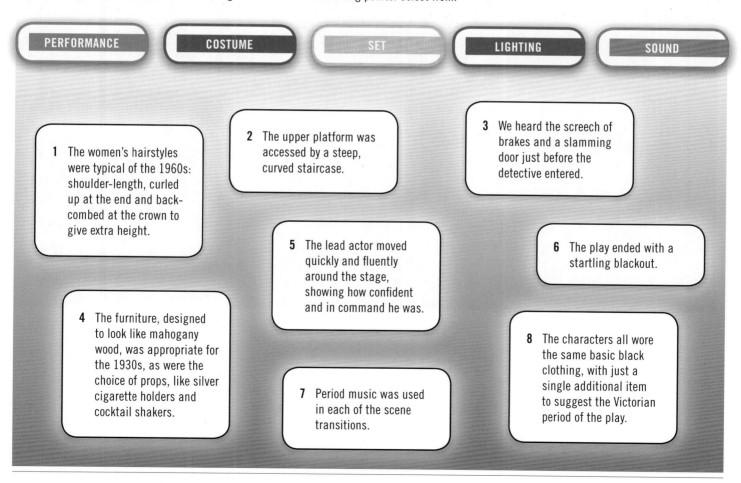

PERFORMANCE   COSTUME   SET   LIGHTING   SOUND

1   The women's hairstyles were typical of the 1960s: shoulder-length, curled up at the end and back-combed at the crown to give extra height.

2   The upper platform was accessed by a steep, curved staircase.

3   We heard the screech of brakes and a slamming door just before the detective entered.

4   The furniture, designed to look like mahogany wood, was appropriate for the 1930s, as were the choice of props, like silver cigarette holders and cocktail shakers.

5   The lead actor moved quickly and fluently around the stage, showing how confident and in command he was.

6   The play ended with a startling blackout.

7   Period music was used in each of the scene transitions.

8   The characters all wore the same basic black clothing, with just a single additional item to suggest the Victorian period of the play.

Task C1

Look at this photograph of an outdoor production of *Robin Hood*.

Make notes on the following:

1 Describe the stage set in detail, including backdrop, levels and use of curtains.

2 Describe the lighting, including the effects and any visible equipment.

3 Pick out any clues about sound.

4 Pick two costumes and describe them in detail, including colours, fabric and silhouette.

5 Note any indications of performance style.

 TIP

In the exam, you will choose to write about either performance skills or one design skill (from a limited selection). Whichever you choose, you must provide detailed examples and use the correct terminology.

 **CHECK IT OUT**

There is a Live Theatre Performance Design Evaluation Sheet on page 176 of *AQA GCSE Drama*, or visit illuminatepublishing.com to download a free copy.

How to write about performance

If you choose to write about the performances you have seen in a show, you should be able to understand the range of skills used by the actors; what they were trying to achieve and how successful they were. You will need to select and include details from the performance to help to explain your ideas and, in doing so, you will need to use correct drama terminology.

Task C2

Study the photographs below and make notes on the following elements of performance, particularly in terms of how they contribute to conveying meaning:

- Facial expression
- Posture
- Stage position
- Use of gesture
- Proximity to other performers.

Also consider what the effect of the performance might be. Does it appear to be comic? Dramatic? Tense?

An open-air production of Dracula

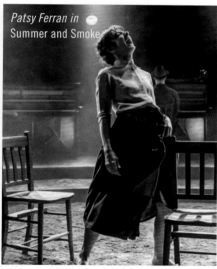

Patsy Ferran in Summer and Smoke

The National Theatre's Nine Night

What the specification says...

Students must develop knowledge and understanding of the following:

▶ How meaning is interpreted and communicated:
  - Use of performance conventions
  - Use of performance space and spatial relationships on stage
  - Relationships between performers and audience
  - Performers' vocal interpretation of character, such as accent, volume, pitch, timing, pace, intonation, phrasing, emotional range, delivery of lines
  - Performers' physical interpretation of character, such as build, age, height, facial features, movement, posture, gesture, facial expression.

TIP

Throughout your exam responses, you must write as an informed drama student and audience member, not just an enthusiastic fan.

Expressing your ideas

When writing about performance skills, it is important that you describe, analyse and evaluate what you have seen, making reference to specific examples from the production.

Although the demands on professional reviewers are different in many ways from those of a drama student, they too have the task of trying to convey the quality of a performance through description and evaluation. Here are excerpts from two reviews of a performance by Patsy Ferran as Alma in *Summer and Smoke* at the Almeida Theatre in 2018:

Reviews of a performance

① Evaluative comment: 'joys'.
② Description of gestures.
③ Analysis of the effect of physical skills.

> One of the joys ① of Ferran's performance is the way her incredibly exact gestures of anxiety – her hand fluttering to her neck, the mystery of what do with one's elbows ② – also so perfectly reveal vast stores of repressed bodily longing.③ She's like a glass, brimming with water; you hold your breath for the moment it'll spill. The moment, of course, comes too late.

Holly Williams, Independent

① Evaluative introduction to overall performance: 'superb'.
② Evaluative comment on vocal skills: 'accent spot-on'.
③ Analysis of impact and precise example.
④ Evaluation: 'beautifully set down'.
⑤ Descriptive comment on vocal skills: 'nervous laugh'.
⑥ Descriptive and notes impact of gestures.
⑦ Analysis of impact of physical skills.
⑧ Descriptive comment on vocal skills: 'cackles', 'top of her voice'.
⑨ Descriptive comment on physical skills.
⑩ Analysis and evaluation of interaction: 'chemistry… off the scale'.

> Ferran is superb, ① her accent spot-on ② – even in its posh elongation of its As which stand her apart from the rest of the town ③ – and her nervousness is beautifully set down. ④ She gulps down air in shallow breaths, has a nervous laugh, ⑤ fiddles with her ring, collar and neck as she tries to talk to the one who is making her heart flutter almost visibly. ⑥ Everything about her performance is subtle but clear… Tension is wound and wound inside her and it bursts out in several separate moments of physical explosion. ⑦ At peak unhappiness she cackles at the top of her voice, ⑧ hyperventilates and stumbles around the stage ⑨. It's like she's a firecracker, waiting to go off, and the chemistry between her and Matthew Needham's John is off the scale. ⑩

Daisy Bowie-Sell, WhatsOnStage

Task C3

Read the following extract from a candidate-style response about the same performance. Use the suggestions for improvement when evaluating your own writing, and then make the necessary changes.

I really liked the actor's performance as Alma. She looked like I thought the character would look and she was both funny and sad. ① She was wearing the same white blouse and dark skirt throughout, which was a bit funny as I thought she should change outfits more because the action took place over several weeks. ② She seemed to like the actor playing the doctor a lot ③ and their scenes together were very interesting. ④ She created an effect ⑤ when she spoke loudly. Sometimes her gestures seemed a bit extreme to me, ⑥ but overall I really liked her work and would like to see her doing more plays. ⑦

① Too general – give examples.

② This is suitable if you chose to write about costume design, but not appropriate for a performance answer.

③ Don't confuse the actor with the character!

④ Why were they interesting? Examples needed.

⑤ What effect was created? Tension? Fear? Humour? Sympathy? Pity?

⑥ What were the gestures and why, in your opinion, didn't they work?

⑦ Concentrate on the performance you saw, rather than general observations.

CHECK IT OUT

See pages 167–174 of *AQA GCSE Drama* for more guidance on writing about performance for Section C.

Aspects of characterisation in performance

Task C4

1 Choose a key character from the play you have seen and write a three-sentence introduction to the character. Include:

- Why the character is important in the play. (Are they the protagonist? Do they provide **comic relief**? Are they the antagonist or villain? Are they a character to whom the audience can relate?)
- The character's status, background and relationships with other characters.
- What the character's motivations are. (What do they want?)

2 Choose three of the sentence starters on the following page and use them in a second paragraph about how the actor portrays the character.

KEY TERM

Comic relief: Light-hearted or humorous characters or interludes that provide a break from more intense, serious sections of a drama.

Meera Syal in Behind the Beautiful Forevers ▲

To examine and discuss a character portrayal, you need to consider how the performer has created the character. In order to do this, you should indicate that you are able to:

▸ understand the character
▸ describe and analyse how the performer used their skills to portray the character
▸ evaluate how successful they were in the portrayal.

Some aspects of characterisation you might consider are the character's:

▸ Status or social background
▸ Relationship with other characters
▸ Personality and/or attitudes
▸ Appearance, including age, gender, height and build
▸ Relationship to their stage environment, including use of stage space and props.

Useful vocabulary for discussing characterisation

You might be asked how an actor has interpreted a role. This means how they have put across their understanding of the playwright's, director's and their own ideas for the character. What aspects of the character has the actor chosen to highlight and what performance techniques are they using to accomplish this? If the actor is interpreting a villainous, comic or romantic character, for example, how have they used their acting skills to do this?

When writing about how a character has been brought to life, you might find that the words offered here will be helpful.

SUBTEXT
The unspoken meaning, feelings and thoughts 'beneath' the lines

MOTIVATION
What a character wants or needs in a scene

STYLE
The manner in which something is performed, such as naturalistically or comically

Sentence starters such as these can help you to structure your writing.

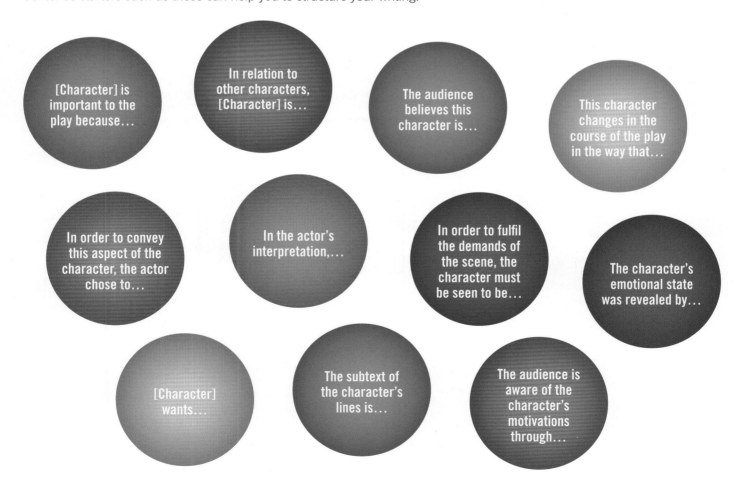

[Character] is important to the play because…

In relation to other characters, [Character] is…

The audience believes this character is…

This character changes in the course of the play in the way that…

In order to convey this aspect of the character, the actor chose to…

In the actor's interpretation,…

In order to fulfil the demands of the scene, the character must be seen to be…

The character's emotional state was revealed by…

[Character] wants…

The subtext of the character's lines is…

The audience is aware of the character's motivations through…

Analysing vocal skills

You might be required to write specifically about vocal techniques either as a named skill, such as 'use of voice', or within the broader term 'acting skills'.

Task C5

1 Experiment with saying the following line of dialogue:

   How dare you speak to me like that.

   Try saying it in the following ways:
   - As the queen, using a firm, commanding tone and an upper-class accent.
   - As a fruit seller on a London market stall, when a customer has been rude to you. Use a Cockney accent, and increased volume.
   - Shocked by what has been said, using a pause and a suprised tone.
   - As a teenager joking around with a friend about something outrageous.

2 Write a paragraph describing in detail the vocal skills you used in part 1 of this task. Analyse what effects you hoped to achieve and evaluate the success of each of your choices.
   - Which words did you emphasise?
   - What was your tone of voice?
   - What volume did you use?
   - How did the use of accent affect how your character might be perceived?
   - What emotion was expressed by your vocal choices?

3 Now try to remember three lines from a play you have seen, and describe, analyse and evaluate in detail how the lines were delivered.

TIP

It is very helpful when writing about vocal skills if you can quote a few lines or words from the play in order to provide precise examples of how vocal skills were used.

Useful vocabulary for discussing vocal skills

When writing about the vocal techniques performers have used, the words and phrases given here will be helpful.

Pitch
The vocal register used (high or low)

Pause
A hesitation or silence

Emotional range
The feelings expressed by the way lines are said

Intonation
The rise and fall of the voice in order to express meaning

Pace
How quickly or slowly the lines are spoken or sung

Emphasis
Stressing or highlighting particular words or phrases

Phrasing
How lines of dialogue are shaped, such as use of hesitation, rhythm, grouping certain words together

Accent
A way of pronouncing words that is associated with a particular country, region or social class

Volume
How loudly or quietly the lines are spoken or sung

Delivery
How lines are said in order to convey meaning

Task C6

Read the following response to a performance and annotate it with the vocal skills being discussed. Use the vocabulary given on the previous page.

> As the music producer, the actor sounded a bit like the Rolling Stones singer Mick Jagger: he drawled certain words and used nasal elongated vowel sounds. This use of a slightly old-fashioned Cockney-type accent associated him with famous rock stars of the 1960s. ① He had excellent comic timing, saying some words very quickly, so that the audience couldn't help but be caught by surprise and laugh at some of his more outrageous lines. He would throw away lines like, 'a genius like me', showing how big his ego was. One scene that particularly showed the actor's skills was when he alternated between talking into his mobile phone and barking instructions at the singer. His use of two different tones was very noticeable, one which was softly intimate changing to one which was commanding and a bit frightening, especially when he said in a cold, matter-of-fact way, 'You're nothing without me.' The emphasis on the word 'nothing' was hard and cruel. This showed how the character was used to controlling people and being obeyed.

① *Accent*

 TIP

If you can, quote two or three lines from the play you have seen in order to give precise examples of how vocal skills are used at a particular point.

Analysing physical skills

In the exam, you might be asked to write about physical skills, either as a named skilled, such as 'use of movement' or under the broader term 'acting skills'.

From the moment an actor appears on stage, you will begin assessing the character they are portraying based on the actor's physical skills, including their:

STANCE AND POSTURE
Straight or hunched, legs together or far apart...

FACIAL EXPRESSIONS
Relaxed or anxious, still or mobile, bland or expressive...

USE OF GESTURES
Powerful or apologetic, calm or frantic, repetitive or varied...

Task C7

1 Experiment with entering a room in different ways. Try out the following scenarios. Imagine you are:
   - A new student in a school and you have arrived late on the first day
   - An army general, getting ready to send your troops into battle
   - Rushing to see a good friend who has returned from a long trip
   - At a ceremony, walking onto a stage to receive a major award.

2 What physical skills did you use in each situation? Make notes on the following for each case:

Use of stage space
Did you use a lot of the space or confine yourself to a small section?

Gestures
Did you use any movements, such as waving to someone or nervously wringing your hands?

Facial expression
Did you smile or grimace? Did you attempt to make eye contact with anyone? Were you tense or relaxed?

Posture
Did you stand upright or were you bent over? Were you leading with a particular part of your body, for example your head, shoulders or feet?

Pace
How quickly or slowly did you move?

Task C8

Choose an entrance that you can remember from a play you have seen. Write about it in detail, noting similar points to those in the previous task.

Useful vocabulary for discussing physical skills

The following terms are useful for writing about performers' physical skills.

MOVEMENT
Changing positions or moving across an area

GESTURES
Small movements that tend to have meaning, such as hand or head movements

USE OF STAGE SPACE
How an actor moves around the stage

CHOREOGRAPHY
Setting movements to music to create dance or other movement sequences

POSTURE
The way a person stands

FACIAL EXPRESSIONS
Emotions (or lack of them) shown on a person's face

INTERACTION WITH OTHERS
How a character reacts to other characters, including movements, physical contact, body language and expressions

STAGE FIGHTS
Blocked movements to safely recreate violence on stage

GAIT
A way of walking

ENTRANCES AND EXITS
How an actor comes on stage or leaves it

HANDLING OF PROPS
Use of portable items, such as walking sticks, books, hand mirrors, brushes and so on

STAGE BUSINESS
Minor movements and/or blocking, such as tidying a room, reading a book or closing a window, in order to establish a situation.

Task C9

Read the performance response given below. Annotate it to show which physical acting skills are being discussed.

In the ghost scene, the actor portrayed both Hamlet and the ghost of his father. This involved very sophisticated use of physical skills. When playing the ghost, he would put on a large overcoat and change his posture, becoming very upright and rigid, ① seeming to grow before our eyes. He would use slow, powerful gestures, such as pointing where Hamlet had previously stood. He also made piercing eye contact with some members of the audience, suggesting his pain and the urgency of his demands. When becoming Hamlet again, the actor would throw off the coat and appear to shrink, his posture becoming hunched and his gestures tentative and fluttering. The transformation was accomplished very quickly, so that the audience was amazed by this **virtuoso** display of physical skills. At the end of the sequence, Hamlet collapsed to the floor as if exhausted.

① Posture

KEY TERM

Virtuoso: Highly skilled; expert in an artistic skill, such as music, dance or acting.

Assessment focus:

▸ *AO3: Demonstrate knowledge and understanding of how drama and theatre is developed and performed*

▸ *AO4: Analyse and evaluate the work of others.*

KEY TERMS

Describe: To give details of what you saw, heard or experienced.

Analyse: To examine something, perhaps by looking at the different elements of it, and to explain it.

Evaluate: To judge or form an opinion, such as explaining what effect was created and how successful it was.

Understanding an exam question about acting

The exact wording of the examination questions will vary from year to year, but you might be asked a question which resembles the one here. Use the notes to help you to think about the detail that will be required.

> **Describe** ① how **one or more actors** in a **particular section** ② of the play used their **acting skills** ③ to create **interesting characters**. ④ **Analyse** ⑤ and **evaluate** how **successful** ⑥ they were in **communicating** their character **to the audience**. ⑦

① Give precise examples so the examiner can picture what you mean.

② 'A particular section', unless otherwise specified, could refer to a single interlude or scene in a play, or could be a longer section, such as a full act. On the other hand, you might be guided to refer to the whole play or to key moments from the play.

③ Acting skills, unless specified, should include both vocal and physical skills.

④ Think about characterisation – instead of 'interesting', other possible wording could include 'believable', 'convincing', 'appropriate', 'effective', 'compelling' and so on.

⑤ To analyse, you need to examine in detail and break down the specific elements, such as use of volume or gesture.

⑥ Did the performers' choices and abilities, in your opinion, work for you and the rest of the audience?

⑦ What impact did the choices and techniques have on the audience and their understanding of the play? You might also be asked to consider how the characterisation contributed to the action, style or genre of the play.

Describing your production and choosing what to write about

It is unlikely that the examiner will have seen the production that you will be writing about. Therefore, your writing must describe the production clearly so that the examiners can understand what you are analysing and evaluating. Examiners are aware that different learning centres will be watching and learning about a variety of plays, so the question they include in the exam must be fairly general. It cannot specify which character or which section of the play you should write about, as the question must suit the wide range of productions seen. It is your responsibility, therefore, to choose a suitable character or characters and an appropriate section of the play about which to write.

◀ *Mimi Ndiweni as Ophelia with Paapa Essiedu as Hamlet, RSC*

Analysis and evaluation

Task C10

Read the following sample candidate-style responses and decide which one contains more analysis and evaluation.

The actor playing Hamlet looked young, pale and thin. He spoke quickly, with a fairly low-pitched voice. Sometimes he would suddenly pause and look out at the audience. He would use gestures, such as grabbing the back of his neck. He was confident about using the whole stage area. He would move quickly from upstage to downstage or climb onto bits of stage furniture. He was very rough when he threw Ophelia to the ground.

The actor's interpretation of Hamlet was a man on the verge of a nervous breakdown. This portrayal was reinforced by his use of vocal skills. At one moment, he would speak fluently and musically, but, in the scene with Ophelia, he appeared both to be 'feigning' madness but also truly distressed. The volume of his voice was at one moment soft and barely audible, then suddenly bursting with anger, such as when he shouted, 'Get thee to the nunnery.' The actor's vocal work was supported by his physical skills, including his hunched, defeated posture from which he would suddenly strike out angrily. His apparent lack of control kept the audience enthralled, wondering what he would do next.

Although the first response describes a number of useful acting skills, it does not analyse why the choices were made nor evaluate the success of them, beyond suggesting that the actor was 'confident'. In the second response, the details are more precise. Phrases such as 'the actor's interpretation' and 'he appears both to be…' suggest analysis, while 'kept the audience enthralled' is evaluative.

 TIP

Remember that, in order to produce a high-quality response, it is important that you don't just describe what you have seen, but that you also analyse why the choices were made and evaluate the effect that they had.

Task C11

1 Write a paragraph describing the acting skills used by one of the actors in a performance you have seen. Then mark:
   - **D** for every description you provide
   - **A** for every analysis when you write about why and how effects were created
   - **E** for every evaluation when you write how successful it was.

2 Read through your paragraph. If you are lacking any of the key elements, rewrite it to make sure you have included examples of description, analysis and evaluation.

Zach Grenier and Lisa Emery in a Broadway production of Gabriel ▲

Choosing key moments from a performance

When discussing performance, you will need to choose which character or characters to write about and from which sections of the play. There is no one right way of doing this, but it is important that you choose a section or key moments that enable you to demonstrate your skills. Particularly interesting moments might be when:

▸ a character is introduced or undergoes a change

▸ a secret is revealed

▸ there is a moment of high emotion

▸ there is a technically difficult demand on the actor (such as a stage fight, multi-rolling, use of disguise or choreography).

An example of a key section: *Gabriel* by Moira Buffini

Gabriel is set on Guernsey in 1943 during the German occupation. Jeanne Becquet, an elegant Guernsey woman, goes out with a Nazi officer whom she believes can only speak German.

The grid below shows how you could begin to choose key moments from a section of a drama in order to analyse and evaluate acting skills.

Key moment	Effects to be achieved	Acting skills used	
Von Pfunz's entrance	Jeanne seems in control of the situation, while Von Pfunz appears comic and foolish	Von Pfunz	• Facial expressions: Open, smiling, not seeming to understand anything. • Gestures/posture: Gallant and formal, opening doors, trying to please.
		Jeanne	• Pace: Moves slowly, gracefully. • Facial expressions: Change between when she thinks Von Pfunz can see her and when she reveals her true feelings. She smiles at Von Pfunz's foolishness when he doesn't seem to understand.
Von Pfunz and Jeanne converse	• Establishing that Von Pfunz seems to speak only German, giving Jeanne freedom to say whatever she likes in English. • Audience will be surprised by how rude she is while pretending to be polite and welcoming.	Von Pfunz	• Accent: The very little English he speaks is highly accented and spoken in a stilted way like a schoolboy reading from a language book. • Pitch: High-pitched giggle, emphasises how comic he is. • Gesture: Wafts his hands, searching for words he seems not to know.
		Jeanne	• Intonation/delivery: The pleasant tone she uses when she speaks is in contrast with the insulting things she says. • Handling of props: Elegant use of cigarette case.
Revelation that Von Pfunz speaks perfect English	• A shock for both the audience and Jeanne that Von Pfunz has understood everything she said. • Changes from a comic scene to something serious and sinister.	Von Pfunz	• Facial expression: Drops open smile – instead looks slyly at Jeanne, with a satisfied grin. • Voice: Speaks perfect, if lightly accented, English. • Posture: Stands upright, assumes high status.
		Jeanne	• Handling of prop: Hides her shock by slowly taking a drink before responding. • Voice: Controls her voice to speak at a steady tempo.

Task C12

Use the format of the grid above to choose key moments from the play you have seen. Make sure that you have chosen a section with enough scope to discuss a variety of acting skills and effects.

Evaluating actors' performances

In order to produce a high-quality response to a question about performance, you will need to make insightful evaluative comments. In order to do this, you could consider:

▸ What were the actors trying to achieve in their performances?
▸ What impact did their acting skills have on the audience?
▸ How did the acting choices contribute to the meaning of the play?
▸ How did the choices contribute to the style of the play?

TIP

A common error is to focus solely on describing what was done without evaluating its effectiveness, particularly in relation to the style of the play. Make sure you check your answers to include this because your ability to 'analyse and evaluate' is assessed in this question.

What are the actors trying to achieve?

- Did they fulfil your expectations of the character, capturing their age, status, occupation and relationship with other characters?
- Did you, from their performance, feel you had an insight into what the character wanted and felt?

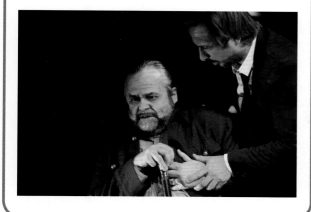

What impact did their acting skills have on the audience?

- Remember, you are an important audience member, so can write about your reactions, as well as those of people around you.
- If it was a comedy, did the audience smile or laugh at appropriate places?
- If it was a tragic piece, was the audience moved at the end?
- Was the audience engaged by the performances?
- Did anything surprise or shock the audience?

How did the acting choices contribute to the meaning of the play?

- Did they create characters who made sense within the period and setting of the play?
- Did they help you to understand the plot and message of the play?

How did the acting choices contribute to the style of the play?

- If it was a slapstick comedy, how did the acting choices add to the humour?
- If it was a highly naturalistic play, how believable were the performances?
- If there were complex movement sequences, were the performers able to deliver these in a slick, professional way?

Useful vocabulary for analysing performance

When writing about how an actor has used their skills, you might find the words and phrases offered here will be helpful.

Making positive evaluative comments

Sentence starters such as these can help you to structure your writing:

▸ The actor contributed to the comedy/tragedy/drama of the piece by…
▸ This caused the audience to…
▸ From this performance, the audience understood…
▸ A powerful choice was…
▸ The actor fully inhabited the character by…
▸ The audience was moved by…
▸ The actor's physical skills made clear…
▸ The actor's use of voice suggested the character's emotions, such as…

Offering constructive criticism

You might see a production in which you feel a performance was disappointing or inadequate. As long as you can analyse why the performance was, in your opinion, unsuccessful, you can explain how you think it could have been improved.

▸ The actor did not fully realise the extreme emotions of the character and…
▸ The performance lacked the necessary…
▸ Although convincing in some sections, at this moment, the performer…
▸ The relationship between the lead characters was disappointing because…
▸ At this key moment, the reactions didn't seem believable because…
▸ Technically, the performance was flawed because… (perhaps it couldn't be heard/seen/understood or did not suit the style or context, for example).
▸ The actor was not well cast in the role because…

Task C13

1 Think of a performance that you were impressed by. Look at the following selection of positive evaluative words and then write a paragraph using at least three of them to discuss a performance you admired (or, if none of these words is appropriate, your own positive adjectives).

convincing comic varied surprising relatable mesmerising thrilling skilful commanding charismatic consistent frightening varied truthful enthralling

2 Think of a performance you have seen which you feel could have been improved. Look at the following selection of words and then write a paragraph using some of them in relation to the performance you are criticising (or use your own critical adjectives).

disappointing unconvincing over-exaggerated awkward unbelievable limited stilted inaudible incomplete monotonous shallow bland repetitive inappropriate inexpressive unemotional

Analysing costume design, including hair and make-up

When writing about the costumes you have seen, you could consider:

- Shape, fit and silhouette
- How the costumes contributed to the style of the play
- How the costumes helped to convey meaning
- How the costumes helped to convey the context of the play
- The choices and use of fabrics and accessories
- Hair and make-up choices and their effect
- How the costumes supported the action
- Colour and texture
- How the costumes helped to portray the characters

In order to prepare for this, it is important to make detailed notes shortly after seeing the production, so that you don't forget vital details. Photographs are also helpful to remind you of details. You can also make additional notes on them during revision.

This photograph is from *The Visit* at the Williamstown Festival Theatre, starring Chita Rivera as Claire Zachanassian. The costume designer was Ann Hould Ward.

> **KEY TERMS**
>
> **Entourage:** A group of people who escort or assist an important person.
>
> **Tragicomic:** A creative work, such as a play or novel, with both tragic and comic elements.

Context: Design suggests an earlier time and fur on clothing suggests a cold location.

Hat: White fur.

Hair: Dark, which contrasts with paleness of face and white outfit. Heavily styled.

Make-up: Pale face, drawing attention to eyes and lips. Bright red lipstick is vivid and suggests an earlier period. Possibly makes her look cruel.

Condition and fit of outfit: As if new and fitting perfectly.

Accessories: Expensive-looking jewellery including 'diamonds' and 'rubies' (indicates wealth).

Long white gloves: gives a sense of old-fashioned formality and perhaps attendance at an exclusive event.

Walking stick: suggests age, frailty.

Sunglasses and white sticks for the entourage: suggesting they are blind.

Colour palette: Mostly contrasting black and white, with striking yellow highlights. White for Claire, which makes her stand out from her entourage and the dark set. The only use of pattern is in the necklace.

Coat: Full length, off-white, silk-type material, with fur collar and cuffs.

Fabric: Fur (fake for costume, but appears genuine: expensive).

Texture: Smooth fabric, complemented with soft, fluffy 'fur'.

Dress: Full length white, empire-line with low bodice, bow detail.

Silhouette: Long coat, suggests late 19th or early 20th century.

Stylised use of highlights, such as yellow platform shoes and the white make-up for two of the characters, suggests a heightened style rather than realism and creates an eerie effect suited to the tragicomic style and message.

Task C14

Look at the photographs below and annotate them with as many points as you can about:

Fabric   Colours   Texture   Silhouette   Make-up

Style   Context   Hair   Accessories   Condition and fit

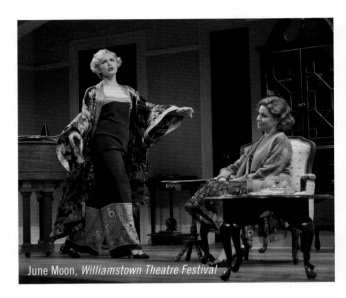

June Moon, *Williamstown Theatre Festival*

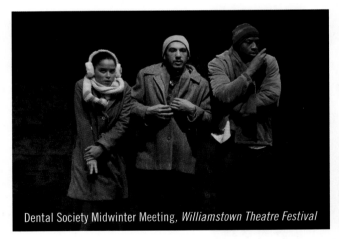

Dental Society Midwinter Meeting, *Williamstown Theatre Festival*

Midnight's Pumpkin, *Kneehigh Theatre, Battersea Arts Centre*

Photo: Steve Tanner / Kneehigh. Designer: Michael Vale

Task C15

Sketch an outline figure and draw in as much detail as you can of a costume you have seen in a play. Annotate it with its various design features as listed in the word bank above.

How costumes contribute to a play's action, style and context

Costumes are not merely decorative additions to a production. The audience expects to be able to 'read' a character partly by what they wear and how they look, and to use the costumes to better understand the play's setting, context and style.

A common error for students in exams is simply to describe costumes rather than analysing how they contribute to the play or evaluating how successful they were.

Task C16

Read the following two responses to the costumes in *The Visit* (shown on page 99). Note any examples of:

- description (D)
- analysis (A)
- evaluation (E).

An example of each has been included for you.

> As Claire is returning to the town for revenge, the designer has created costumes which emphasise her wealth. Ⓐ The costume designer, Ann Hould Ward, has dressed Claire entirely in white, which contrasts both with the dark colours worn by her male entourage, but also with the poor clothes of the inhabitants of the town. Her clothes fit perfectly and are in pristine condition – highlighted by their shiny, spotless whiteness, whereas the townspeople's costumes are dull, shabby, mended and loose-fitting Ⓓ. The fabrics used further emphasise her wealth – the white coat suggests the finest silk, while the trim is fur, such as might be found on an Arctic fox. When she is on stage, it is impossible to take your eyes off Claire, which is surely the effect the designer wanted.

> The style of the production is tragicomic and, at times, expressionistic. It is also a musical, so the costumes have been designed so that the performers can move easily in them. Rivera, as Claire, can remove the coat, so that the empire line flowing dress underneath allows for more movement and gives her a more fluent silhouette. The blinded entourage figures are both eerie and comic. They are dressed identically to emphasise that they work as a team. Their outfits combine conventional black suits and bowler hats with stylistic effects, such as the white-face masks and yellow shoes. The effect is to remove any sense of their individuality. This succeeds Ⓔ in making the audience accept Claire's cruelty more easily.

Task C17

1 Write one paragraph about one or more costumes in a play you have seen. Explain how the costumes support the play's style, plot and/or context.

2 Afterwards, read your work to check that you have included description, analysis and evaluation.

 TIP

There is no one 'right' answer to this question. Both of the sample responses here are strong, although they make different points about the costumes in *The Visit*.

KEY TERMS

Pristine: As if new; perfect; clean.

Expressionistic: A non-naturalistic style that highlights subjective emotions.

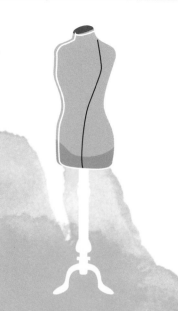

Deciding what to write about costumes

You might see a production in which there are dozens of exciting costumes that you could write about. Avoid the temptation to try to write about them all. In the time you have available in the exam, it is far better to write in detail about a limited number of costumes.

The grid below offers one way to make notes about costumes. Once you have completed a grid like this for the show you have seen, you will find it easier to select those costumes about which you have the most to say.

 **CHECK IT OUT**

Page 178 of *AQA GCSE Drama* has more samples of student-style responses on costume design.

 TIP

Remember to consider if a costume is changed or altered in the course of the play. What are the effects of the changes?

Detailed costume description	What the costume communicates about character, plot, style and context	How the costume is used in the play	How effective it is
• Naturalistic period costume. • Secretary's costume: – 1930s navy blue dress. White collar, high neckline. Below the knee. Light wool fabric. – Matching coat, with belt. – Cloche hat. – Low-heeled strap shoes. – Simple necklace and small gold earrings.	• The character is prim and proper, contrasting with the more flamboyant wife, who usually wears red. • The period is reflected in the style of dress and fabric used, as well as the distinctive hat: the style is clearly early 20th century.	• The character puts on a hat and coat when she vows to leave her boss. • The low-heeled leather shoes fit her practical personality, but also make it possible for the actor to perform the choreography.	The outfit was partially successful. It perhaps looked a little too worn and dowdy in the office scenes, considering she is meant to be a love rival to the wife, but the transformation when she put on the hat and coat were effective – she suddenly looked like an interesting, independent businesswoman in her own right.
• Stylised modern costume. • Cardboard was used in many costumes, including being taped on the soldiers to serve as armour or shaped into large rigid skirts for the women. These items were placed over the loose grey cotton trousers and T-shirts they otherwise were wearing.	• The play was set in a refugee camp where the performers appeared to use the resources around them to create costumes. • Besides cardboard, other materials, all made from easily available items, included: – gaffer tape – crayons to add decoration and colour – black bin bags for draping – tin cans.	There were short interludes when characters would be seen on stage fashioning a costume on others, leading to the performer gradually acquiring the costume that suited their character.	Using 'found' items to create the costumes was continually interesting and creative. The queen's costume was particularly successful. It involved a pleated cardboard skirt, a draped bin-liner bodice and a crown fashioned from a tin can. She seemed to be at once a refugee and a proud queen.

Useful vocabulary for describing and discussing costumes

When writing about the details of costumes, including headwear, hairstyles and make-up, you might find the following example words and phrases helpful.

Fabric

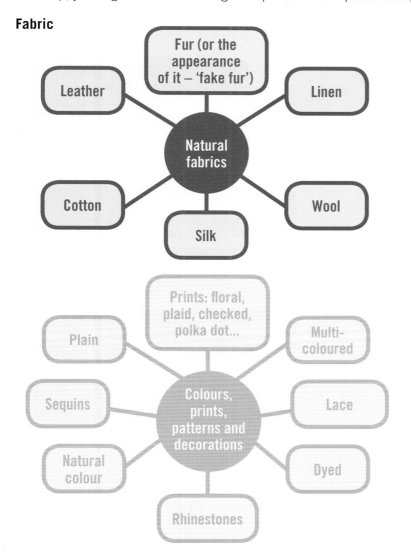

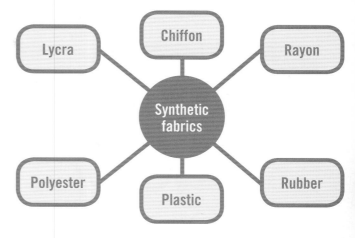

Fit and condition

Silhouette

Hourglass: Tightly fitted to create a small waist and fullness at hips and bust. Associated with women's clothing, particularly in periods such as the Victorian era or mid-20th century.

Empire line: Cut with a high waist (typically just under the bust), a low neckline and long, draping skirt. Associated with the late 18th to early 20th centuries.

Drop waist: A dress with a low waistline. These usually hang loosely from shoulder to hip, with a loose pleated or gathered skirt from the hip to the knee. Particularly associated with the 1920s.

Corsetry: Undergarments such as corsets, girdles and bustles used to shape a body and alter its silhouette.

Exaggerated: Emphasising one area of the body. An example is large shoulder pads, popular in 1940s suits, to give a triangular shape to the body.

Slim: Long, streamlined garments, favoured in many periods including the 18th century, the 1920s and the 1960s.

COMPONENT 1 UNDERSTANDING DRAMA

Colour

Colour palette: The range of colours used. For example, a limited palette would only include a few colours.

Colour coding: Using colours to indicate something about characters, such as a family group or to suggest a character's transition by moving from muted tones to bright colours.

Padding

Protective padding: Clothing with extra cushioning to protect performers in difficult or dangerous physical tasks.

Shoulder padding: Pads or extra material at the shoulders to create a broad-shouldered silhouette.

Character padding: To add weight to or change the shape of a character, such as with a 'pregnancy belly' or 'humpback'.

Footwear

Style and features: Straps, Boots, Sandals, Lace-ups, Brogues, Buckles, Ribbons, Loafers, Slippers, Laces, Stitching, Trainers

Decorative details

Buttons: Size, colour, plain or decorative.

Embroidery: Decorative stitching.

Braid: Woven cord or other fabrics, such a gold braid added to a jacket.

Trim: Additional decorative items such as fur on the collar or cuffs of a jacket or a fringe on a skirt.

Style

Period/historical: Designed to replicate or suggest a particular time period.

Fantastical/stylised: Designed to suggest non-naturalistic characters or situations, such as representing animals, inanimate objects or futuristic, exaggerated, abstract or symbolic figures.

Modern/contemporary: Representing current fashions and trends.

Hats

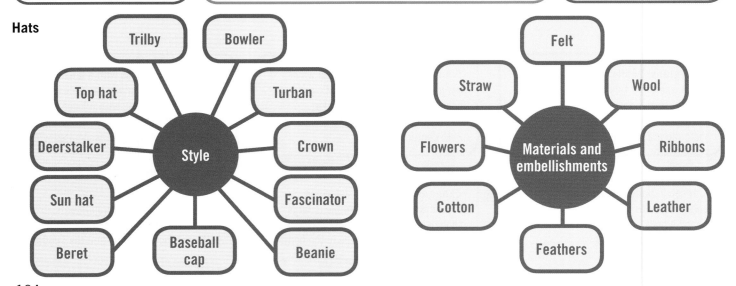

Style: Trilby, Bowler, Top hat, Turban, Deerstalker, Crown, Sun hat, Fascinator, Beret, Baseball cap, Beanie

Materials and embellishments: Felt, Straw, Wool, Flowers, Ribbons, Cotton, Leather, Feathers

Hair

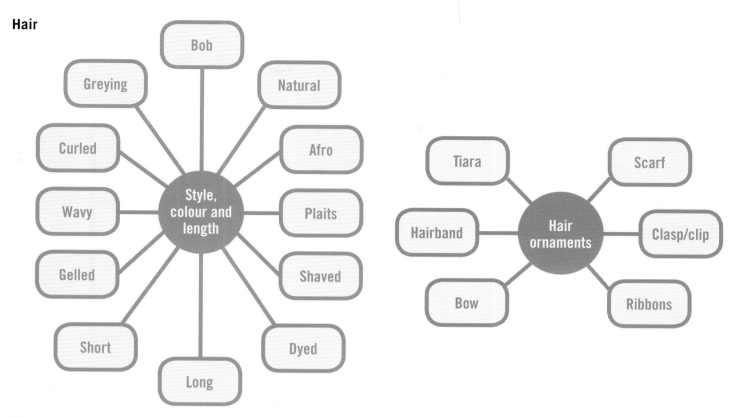

Wigs

Natural: Appears to be the actor's own hair, but might add length or suggest a particular style or period.

Theatrical: Stylised or exaggerated, for example, incorporating unusual colours or shapes.

Period: To recreate certain historic periods or to replicate the sorts of wigs worn by people in different times, such as an 18th-century powdered wig.

Make-up

Basic or straight: Designed to look natural.

Character: Used to significantly alter an actor's appearance.

Prosthetics: Additional pieces that can be attached, such as false noses, artificial wounds or horns.

Stylised: Face-painting, animal make-up, mime or clown make-up.

Ageing make-up: Shadows and lines.

Facial hair

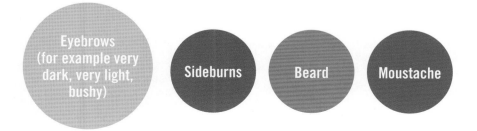

Task C18

Refer to either a production you have seen or to one of the photographs on page 100, and write a paragraph to discuss the costume, hair and make-up. Use at least six of the words or phrases given on these pages.

Analysing set design

When writing about the set and prop design of the play you have seen, consider:

TIP

There will be three options for Section C in the exam. If one of the questions is about set design, it could be something like the following.

'Describe how the set was used to help the audience understand the style and action of the play.

Analyse and evaluate how successful they were in creating an interesting and effective set.'

You might want to write about:

- the use of space, levels and scale
- colours, textures and materials.

Remember that the question will be worth 32 marks.

▸ How the set helped to communicate meaning
▸ How the set contributed to the style of the play
▸ What the set and props conveyed about the characters and context
▸ How the set and props helped the action
▸ How the set and props contributed to mood or atmosphere
▸ The staging configuration
▸ Any essential or particularly interesting furnishings, dressings and props
▸ The colours, textures and materials used in the set
▸ Any backdrops, flats or projections
▸ Whether one set was used or if there were set changes or a composite set
▸ Any levels, ramps or staircases
▸ Where entrances and exits occurred.

The photograph on the following page shows a scene from a 2013 production of *Pygmalion*, designed by Alexander Dodge and set in the early 20th century.

LOOK HERE

See pages 127, 128 and 137 for more Section C exam-type questions.

Task C19

After studying the *Pygmalion* set and its accompanying annotations, answer the following questions.

1 How does the set convey the period of the play?

2 What does the set suggest about the character who owns this room, Henry Higgins? What are likely to be his interests, his social position and his personality?

3 What effect do you think this set would have on the audience? Would they be impressed by it? Interested in what happens in this space? Curious about the characters who live in this space?

A traditional period set for *Pygmalion*

Fabrics: Leather sofa, wooden furniture, wool carpet

Set dressings: Portraits, art, books

Floor covering: Geometric-patterned, yellow-toned carpet

Stage furnishings: Small leather sofa centre stage. Small table and two wooden chairs stage right. Cushioned footstool stage left. Wooden chair stage left. Desk and chair upstage centre. Cabinets along upstage wall.

Wall coverings: Elaborate, bold leaf-pattern, period wallpaper

Set changes: Five acts in the play involve five set changes, including an outdoor scene in Covent Garden, Mrs Higgins' drawing room and this set of Professor Higgins' study.

Staging configuration: End on

Texture: Most surfaces are smooth. Room appears clean but cluttered

Levels: Small staircase/ladder leading to pipe organ on upper platform

Context: Edwardian period

Entrances/exits: Five doors: one upstage right, two stage right and two stage left

Style of set: Naturalistic, box set

Colours: Green, white and purple wallpaper. Yellow and blue carpet. Light- and mid-brown wood

A modern set for *For the Lulz*

Below is a modern, **minimalist** set for a play called *For the Lulz* about a computer hacker who attacks social networks.

Set changes: One set is used to suggest several different locations, with stage furnishing, such as a desk, brought on and off as necessary.

Colours: Dark, with black floor and background, as well as black chairs. The red and green design on the floor breaks up the darkness.

Staging configuration: Thrust

Style: Minimalistic, non-naturalistic

Context: Modern, contemporary

Backdrop/flats: Black flat with projections

Floor coverings: Black floor with green lines (tape) and red dots. Geometric appearance. Might suggest the workings of the Internet.

Entrances/exits: Can occur through audience or from upstage. No practical doors appear in the set.

Stage furnishings: Black office chair on castors, laptop

KEY TERM

Minimalist: Simple, spare; using few elements; stripped back.

Task C20

Read the annotations around the photograph and then answer these questions.

1 How does the set design reinforce the issues of hacking and social media explored in the play?
2 How can the audience tell from the design that this is a modern play discussing contemporary issues?
3 What mood or atmosphere is established by the set?
4 What aspects of the set design do you think might intrigue the audience?

An expansive outdoor set for *Lord of the Flies*

Task C21

Look closely at this photograph of an outdoor production of *Lord of the Flies* at Regent's Park Open Air Theatre.

Make detailed notes, like those on the photographs on the previous pages, about its set design.

Task C22

Draw a detailed sketch of the set in the production you watched. If it had any complete set changes, draw separate sketches to show each complete set.

On your sketches, note:
* Staging configuration
* Colours, fabrics and textures used
* Any stage furnishings and props
* How scene changes occurred
* Levels, entrances and exits.

 **CHECK IT OUT**

See pages 179–180 of *AQA GCSE Drama* for more ideas about analysing and evaluating sets.

How set design contributes to action, style and context

Many theatrical productions do not use curtains, so audiences might see some or all of the set when they first walk into the auditorium. You might, therefore, have an instant impression of the production you are going to see and you might begin to make judgements about it. You could see a play with an expensive, complex set or a simpler minimalistic set or a single naturalistic set. Whatever play you see, you must be able to identify the choices the set designer has made and how they help to convey the play's meaning.

TIP

A common error in the exam is simply to describe the set design rather than analysing how it contributes to the play or evaluating how successful it was. Remember to include analysis and evaluation.

Task C23

Read the following samples of candidate-style responses about two set designs for two different productions. Note any examples of:

- description (D)
- analysis (A)
- evaluation (E).

Ⓓ Description of style.

The set of <u>Summer and Smoke</u>, designed by Tom Scutt, was not the naturalistic type of set many associate with the work of playwright Tennessee Williams. Instead, the design was minimalistic Ⓓ and stripped back, showing the bare brick walls of the theatre and a plain floor. Two steps up from the main acting area was a semi-circle of nine pianos around the acting space. These pianos were used by the actors to create music, but also to represent Alma's love of the arts. This choice was highly effective because it removed the clutter which often accompanies naturalistic plays and put the focus on the characters, particularly Alma. The pianos also added excitement to the staging, as actors would perch on top or walk across them or sit down to play them, creating a soundtrack.

Ⓐ Analysis of what the set had to achieve.

The set of <u>Sunset Boulevard</u> recreated Hollywood of the early 20th century. The designer had the difficult task of creating a range of complex sets which had to be moved quickly into place to suggest new locations. Ⓐ Also, as this was a touring production, the set had to fit a wide range of theatres. Norma Desmond's house, with its grand staircase and yellow velvet sofa suggested an earlier era which contrasted with the bright casual diner set where the studio workers met and partied. This made clear the choice Joe would have to make – the dark past with Norma or the bright future with Betty. One element of the design which divided opinion was the use of an incomplete prop-type car. While some didn't like it as it distanced them from the impending tragedy, I felt it worked well because it reflected Norma's inability to separate fantasy from reality. The use of projected films, including Norma as a young girl, was also successful as it reinforced the play's preoccupation with film-making and the distance between Norma as a young woman and how she now appeared.

Task C24

Consider the set for a production you have seen and write a paragraph about how it was used to support the play's style, context and action. Afterwards, check over your work, making sure you have described (D), analysed (A) and evaluated (E).

Useful vocabulary for discussing set designs

Using technical terminology correctly will help you to produce high-quality writing. It is unlikely that the production you will see will use all of the following, but see if any can be included in your practice writing about set design.

Backdrop
A large painted cloth hung as part of the scenery.

Flat
A piece of scenery mounted on a frame.

Multimedia
Use of film or other media during the production.

Scrims
Gauze stage curtains which, depending how they are lit, can either be opaque or translucent.

Trapdoor
A door in the floor of a stage allowing objects or performers to be dropped, lifted or lowered.

Cyclorama
A large semi-circular stretched curtain or screen, usually positioned upstage. This is often used to depict a background, such as the sky.

Fly system
A means of raising and lowering scenery or other items onto the stage using a system of ropes and pulleys. You can refer to 'flying a set in'.

Projection
Projecting a film or still image to form a theatrical backdrop.

Set dressings
Items on the set not actually used as props, but that create detail and interest, such as vases or framed paintings.

Truck
A platform on wheels upon which scenery can be mounted and moved.

Drapes
Curtains or other hanging fabric.

Furnishings
Furniture on the set, such as chairs, cushions and tables.

Revolve
A large turntable device that can be turned to reveal a different setting.

Symbolic
Using something to represent something else. A symbolic stage set might be a non-naturalistic design to suggest something about the play and its themes, such as a heavy use of red to suggest violence, or a house wall with a crack down its middle to suggest a family torn apart.

Wing space
An area to the side of the stage from which actors can enter and from which props, furnishings or sets can be moved onto the stage.

Task C25

Check your notes on the production you have seen and highlight any of the terms above that could be used to explain and discuss in a technically accurate way what you have seen.

Analysing lighting design

Below is an example of stage lighting from the Company One production of *Shockheaded Peter*.

Floor lights and footlights used to create uplighting and shadows.

Low intensity wash of light on stage keeps all figures lit to some degree.

Red filter used (particularly seen on central figure's forehead).

Shadows on back wall create eerie, frightening effect.

Two figures in the foreground are lit with the most intensity.

Uplighting casts shadows on faces, particularly under eyes of central figure.

Footlights contribute to Victorian period and music-hall feel of the design.

A different use of lighting is seen in *The Old Man and the Old Moon* where PigPen Theatre Company use storytelling techniques in their plays.

Intense backlighting used to create shadow puppet effect.

Sections of the stage in darkness.

Sources of lighting are not hidden, but are part of the performance.

Performer also uses portable handheld light.

Lighting colours: golden yellow.

Uplighting, probably from a floor light, casts light on the storyteller's face.

Task C26

Make detailed notes about the lighting in a production you have seen, including:

- Is lighting subtle or noticeable?
- How are transitions handled? Are there blackouts? Fades? Cross-fades?
- Are the sources of light visible or hidden?
- What colours of lighting are used?
- Are there any special effects created by lighting?
- Is there any particular focusing of light, on a face or prop, for example?
- Can you see examples of different uses of light?
- How are the lighting effects created, do you think?
- Are there key moments when lighting is used particularly noticeably or effectively?

Choosing key moments where lighting is important

Use a grid like the one below to select key lighting states and transitions and to evaluate how effective they were in the production you watched.

Lighting state/transition	Description	Evaluation
At the opening of the play, a sunlit drawing room in an English country house	<ul><li>House lights dim and stage lights fade up to reveal room.</li><li>Golden/orange light, probably from a fresnel lantern in the wings, angled down to recreate effect of light streaming through the window.</li><li>General wash of light in the rest of the room.</li><li>Midway through the scene, an actor 'turns on' a desk lamp.</li><li>Gradual fade down of window and general wash lights at the end of the scene.</li></ul>	<ul><li>The lighting is successful in recreating a naturalistic English country setting, with the attractive light adding to the feeling of wealth and comfort of the family.</li><li>The use of onstage, visible lighting, such as the desk lamp appearing to be operated by actors, adds to the naturalism. This also highlights that it is getting late.</li></ul>
Transition between scenes	Between each episode of the play, two very bright tubes of light attached to two screens would appear. The shape of the lights had the appearance of fluorescent lamps, but, given their intensity, were probably LED lights. The tubes would suddenly flash, almost blinding the audience.	The effect was very disorienting. You could see the audience was shocked and made uncomfortable by the bright light. The technique signalled a sharp ending to each scene and meant that the audience's identification with the emotion of the previous scene was cut off before the next scene began.

 **CHECK IT OUT**

See pages 182–183 of *AQA GCSE Drama* for more examples of lighting analysis and evaluation.

How lighting contributes to a play's action, style and context

Your writing about lighting in live theatre should show that you understand how lighting contributed to the overall production. The lighting demands of a big musical, for example, will be very different from that of an intimate, minimalistic play. Some designs might simply indicate the beginning and end of scenes or the time of day; while others will have a wide variety of special effects.

A fresnel lantern with barn doors ▲

KEY TERMS

Barn doors: Metal flaps used on fresnel lanterns to shape the light beam into, for example, a square. They also lessen the 'spill' of light, ensuring that a precise area is lit.

Strobe: A lighting device that produces short bursts of light.

Task C28

Write two paragraphs about the lighting design in a production you have seen. Look over what you have written and mark examples of description, analysis and evaluation. If any are missing, go back and edit. Try to include some of the terms given on the following page.

Task C27

Read the following samples of candidate-style responses about two lighting designs. Note any examples of:

- description (D) • analysis (A) • evaluation (E).

> The lighting had an important role to play. The set was minimalistic, so the lighting established the location, time of day and mood of each scene. Instead of employing a general wash of light across the stage, the designer used a combination of profile and fresnel lanterns to focus attention on particular areas of the stage. Barn doors were used on the fresnel lanterns to restrict the spill of light and shape the illumination into tight rectangles, which suggested the claustrophobia of the cabin's rooms. The lighting added to the mystery and tension of the play, as you never knew where you would need to look next. Ⓐ One particularly effective section was the scene when a gentle white light streamed in diagonally from upstage left to suggest the light from a kitchen window as a woman washed dishes. The mood was calm. Then suddenly a pinpoint high-intensity green light snapped onto a strange woman's face outside the window, which made us jump with surprise.

> Colour was important in this lighting design. This was particularly noticeable in the fight scene when red filters were introduced and increased in intensity and brightness as the gangs approached each other. When the physical altercation occurred, a **strobe** was employed. The effect was to plant a series of suspenseful still images in the audience's mind which occurred so quickly we could barely take them in. There would be a flash of light and we would see the group in a huddle, with Joe's arm outstretched. The next flash revealed a knife. Another showed the group pulling away from the centre. The last revealed Joe, apparently dead, on the ground centre stage, in the pool of an intense white spotlight beaming directly down from the lighting rig in the flies. Although it was undoubtedly an exciting use of light, I felt that using red to show violence was a little clichéd, but judging by the audience silence at the end of the sequence, it was clearly effective for others.

Useful vocabulary for discussing lighting design

Backlight
Light projected from a source upstage. It highlights the outline of actors or scenery and separates them from the background. It can also create sculptural effects.

Barn doors
Metal flaps used on fresnel lanterns to make the beam into a particular shape, such as a square. They also lessen the 'spill' of light.

TIP

A common exam error is simply to describe the lighting design. Remember to analyse how it contributed to the play and evaluate how successful it was.

Blackout
Switching off all stage lights. This can be sudden or gradual.

Black hole
An area of the stage accidentally left unlit.

Colour filter
Coloured pieces of plastic on a lantern that alter the colour of the light. Also called 'gels'.

Cross-fade
A transition in which lighting states are changed by bringing up the new state while reducing the old state.

Fade
To gradually bring up (fade up) or diminish lights (fade down).

Floodlight
A lantern without a lens, which produces an unfocused wash of light.

Floor lights
Lanterns on low stands, often used to cast shadows.

Fluorescent
Tubular lights used to efficiently and inexpensively light large areas. (Frequently used in schools, warehouses and factories.)

Focus
How tightly or sharply defined a beam of light is, such as a well-focused circle or square.

Followspot
A powerful spotlight operated so that its beam follows an actor around the stage.

Footlights
Low lights placed on the downstage front edge of the stage. These were popular in Victorian theatre and musical halls and are sometimes used to create period lighting effects.

Fresnel
A lantern with a lens that produces a soft-edged beam of light.

Gobo
A metal cut-out used to project patterns, such as leaves, stars, swirls or waves.

House lights
The lights in the auditorium that are usually on while the audience is being seated and turned off as the performance is about to begin.

LED stage lighting
LED stands for 'light-emitting diode'. LEDs can be very powerful and colourful (without using gels) and are energy-efficient. They are unable, however, to create some effects used in traditional stage lighting, such as hard-edged beams.

Neon
Bright gas-filled tubes of light that are frequently used in electric signs.

Pinspot
A spotlight so tightly focused it only lights a very small area, such as a single object or an actor's face.

Profile
A type of lantern with a lens that can project clear outlines.

Smoke or haze machine
A machine that produces clouds or mist.

Strobe
A lighting device that gives short bursts of lighting.

Wash
Lighting that covers the whole stage.

Analysing sound design

When writing about sound design you might consider:

▶ Whether the sound design was naturalistic or abstract

▶ How the sound design contributed to the style of the play

▶ If sound contributed to the plot and action of the play

▶ If the sound design clarified the context or location of the play

▶ How sound helped to create certain moods or atmosphere

▶ How sound effects were accomplished

▶ If sound was amplified or distorted

▶ Whether sound effects were live or recorded

▶ What music was used

▶ If the use of sound affected the action on stage, such as actors moving in time with music

▶ Whether the sounds had an impact on the audience. Did the audience react to any sounds? Did the use of sound create tension or humour?

You might see a production which has sound and music at its heart. *The Dixon Family Album*, below, for example, uses actor-musicians to trace the fortunes of a folk music group in the 1960s.

Context: 1960s folk music, reinforces setting.

Singing: Actors sing on stage.

Actor-musicians: Instruments played live on-stage.

Microphones: General-use microphones on stands to amplify singing and musical instruments.

Offstage: Drummer and additional sound equipment offstage left.

Some productions will make particular demands upon a sound designer, for example, if they occur in unusual places, such as outdoors, where the acoustics might be difficult. In the scene shown on the following page, from *Gigi* at Regent's Park Open Air Theatre, the performers are singing, and dancing to music, which contributes to the cheerful mood of the scene. Consider, however, how the outdoor setting means that speakers and microphones must be carefully placed and used, and that sound balancing can be difficult.

On the other hand, you might have seen a production which uses music in a subtle way, **subliminally** affecting the audience's mood. Or you might have seen a production in which naturalistic sound effects are important for the plot, such as gunshots, animal noises, crowds, traffic or alarms.

Task C29

Make detailed notes on the sound design of the production you have seen, using the bullet points on the previous page.

Choosing key moments of the use of sound

Use a grid like the one below to help you to select a suitable section of the production you have seen in order to describe, analyse and evaluate the sound design effectively.

Description of sound	Analysis of how it was achieved	Evaluation of its effect and impact
The sound of a slow metronome as the characters waited for the jury's verdict	This sound was recorded and then amplified on speakers that surrounded the stage. It snapped on and off.	The tick of the metronome was used to emphasise the tension of the long wait for judgement. It played for at least a minute, but seemed longer, especially as there was no other sound, creating significant tension for the audience and a sense of surprise when it suddenly stopped.

KEY TERM

Subliminally: In a way that barely registers: the audience is affected without consciously being aware of what is affecting them.

 TIP

If you choose to write about sound design for this section, you must ensure that you have seen a production which offers enough scope for you to be able to write thoroughly about the design. If you have seen a production with only one sound effect or a couple of minor music cues, you might find it difficult to write enough.

 **CHECK IT OUT**

See page 181 of *AQA GCSE Drama* for more advice on how to analyse and evaluate sound.

TIP

A common error in the exam is just to describe the sound design. Remember to include analysis of how it contributed to the play and evaluation of how successful it was.

How sound design contributes to action, style and context

Your writing about sound design in live theatre should show that you understand how sound contributes to the overall production. The sound demands of a big musical with a specially composed score and large orchestra, for example, will be very different from that of an intimate, minimalistic play with a few recorded sound effects. The use of sound might include effects created on stage, recorded sound effects or original music composition.

Task C30

Read the following samples of candidate-style responses about sound design in two different productions. Note any examples of:

- description (D)
- analysis (A)
- evaluation (E).

(D) Description of how sound assists the style of the play

In this production of <u>The Caucasian Chalk Circle</u> by Bertolt Brecht, the sound designer used sound to contribute to the epic style of the play. (D) Brecht believed that the audience should not think they are watching real-life and used the alienation effect to remind them they were in a theatre watching actors. The sound design supported this, by showing the actors setting up microphone stands and testing microphones as the audience came in. In the scene by the river, an actor placed a general-use microphone on a low stand next to a bowl of water and created the splashing noises next to the actors enacting the scene. This added to the artificiality of the play's style. Additionally, all the actors played instruments (guitar, drums, tambourine, violin) and sang music which had been specially composed for this performance. This was always done in view of the audience, with the musicians either at the centre of the action or sitting downstage, watching the action. The music was more modern (rock rather than folk) and relevant to the audience than the style more usually associated with Brecht's plays.

KEY TERMS

Epic: A type of early 20th-century theatre particularly associated with Bertolt Brecht. It is non-naturalistic theatre that uses particular techniques to remind the audience they are watching a play.

Alienation effect: A distancing effect that prevents the audience from believing they are watching a real event. It might involve breaking the fourth wall by speaking directly to the audience or drawing attention to the mechanics behind the play's production.

Task continued on next page ▶

In this play, set in an Internet chatroom, music played a vital role. The audience was immediately startled when the characters entered to a recording of the Oompa Loompa song from the 1971 Willy Wonka film. The volume was loud, with speakers at the front of the stage blasting the song out as the actors, dressed in ordinary contemporary clothes, but moving rigidly in time with the music, entered. The effect was odd, making the audience laugh and preparing them for a play which would surprise them repeatedly. The song snapped off and the actors seamlessly began their dialogue. To reinforce the setting, the sound design incorporated a range of recorded notification 'pings' and 'whoosh' sound effects to punctuate the characters' online debates. At the end of the first scene, there was loud burst of the Prodigy's 'Firestarter' song, approximately 20 seconds, which accompanied the actors' '**chairography**' as they positioned the chairs for the next scene. This use of sound and music made the production seem modern and relevant, as well as keeping the pace high. (A) Additionally, the choice of 'Firestarter' added a sense of danger.

(A) Analysis of how important sound was to establishing the location and period of the play

KEY TERM

Chairography: Choreographed movement involving moving or rearranging chairs on the stage.

Task C31

Consider this exam-style question:

'Describe how sound was used in the production to create mood and/or atmosphere. Analyse and evaluate how successful the sound design was in affecting the audience's experience and understanding of the play. You could make reference to:

- the use of sound effects and music, including any special techniques
- how and at what level the sound is projected and amplified
- a notable section of the play or the play as a whole.'

In response, write two paragraphs about the sound design for a section of the play you have seen. Afterwards, go over your writing, noting when you have:

- described (D)
- analysed (A)
- evaluated (E).

If you are missing any of these, rewrite the paragraphs to make sure you can include them.

Useful vocabulary for discussing sound design

Abstract
Symbolic, not realistic, such as a loud beating heart for tension or dripping water to suggest the passing of time.

Actor-musicians
Performers who play musical instruments as part of their acting roles.

Acoustics
The sound quality in a space, such as whether an auditorium affects sound by making it clear, echoing, warm or muffled and so on.

Composer
Someone who writes music. For some productions, a composer will create original music.

Curtain-call music
Music played during curtain call. Sometimes the curtain call is choreographed to a particular song.

Fade
To gradually turn sound up or down.

Live sounds
Sound created either by the stage management, technicians or actors during the performance. In some productions, where the theatricality of the performance is being highlighted, the sound effects are created in front of the audience.

Microphones
These pick up sound for amplification and might be:
- body-worn: worn by the actors
- general use: placed near the source of a sound
- directional: placed at a distance from the source of the sound
- overheads: hung above the stage to boost the overall sound.

Motivated sound
Sound effects required by the script, particularly in terms of plot and action, such as a gunshot or an alarm.

Musical instruments
Drums, guitars, violins and so on which might be played by a band, orchestra or by the actors.

Musical theme or motif
A distinctive recurring section of music. In sound design, it might be associated with a particular character or mood.

Naturalistic
Realistic sound effects, such as traffic, birdsong, crowds.

Pre-show music
Music played as the audience enters and waits for the performance to begin.

Recorded sound
Played-back sound that might have been recorded specially for the performance or found in sound effects archives.

Reverb
(From 'reverberation'.) An echoing effect, sustaining the sound longer than usual.

Snap
To turn a sound suddenly off or on.

Sound effects (SFX)
Special sounds created either through using recorded effects, such as birdsong and traffic, or creating them live, such as a door slamming or offstage voices.

Speakers
The means of amplifying the sound. The placement of the speakers will influence how the audience experiences the sound.

Transitions/scene changes
How music or sound is used during transitions or scene changes, such as to establish a new location or mood.

Volume
How loud or soft a sound or voice is.

TEST YOURSELF C2

Read these responses to different productions and identify whether they are about **performance**, **sound**, **lighting**, **costume** or **set**. Also consider if they describe, analyse or evaluate.

1. The use of a revolve contributed greatly to the excitement of the party scene. As it slowly turned, the set revealed a new room in the house. As the party continued, the rooms became more and more cluttered, suggesting that the party was getting out of hand.

2. From the actor's first entrance, the audience was captivated. To create the recklessness of his character, he hurtled onto the stage, appearing to be wild and, judging by the bottle he was holding, drunk. He suddenly stopped and smiled, enjoying the impression he had made on both the other characters and, slyly, the audience.

3. The use of music from the 1950s highlighted the period of the play.

6. A pinpoint spotlight closed in on the actor's face, showing her distressed expression, followed by a sudden blackout that left the audience shocked.

4. The uniform established the character's status, as well as his appeal to the women of the town. The close-fitting scarlet jacket, with gold braid trim, made him stand out from the other characters who were generally dressed in muted greys, greens and browns.

5. The actors' German accents were truly impressive.

7. As a major theme was women's beauty, the designer had made the three-storey set resemble a beauty counter: white smooth reflective, curved surfaces, racks of pastel products and a large white surface upon which advertisements could be projected.

8. Whenever the children entered, a gentle piece of piano music accompanied them, making their scenes seem almost dream-like.

9. The audience jumped at the unexpected explosion at the end of Act 1. The speakers were positioned all around the auditorium, creating the effect that we too were caught up in the blast.

10. The outfits were stylised and extravagant: primary colours, exaggerated silhouettes and rich fabrics and decorations.

12. A speaker at the back of the auditorium was used to project the sound of a car driving along a gravel drive.

11. Columns of lights descended from the fly space. The mystery of the effect was increased by the use of a haze machine, making the light seem thick, like mist.

 **TEST YOURSELF C3**

Match the correct definition with the technical production term.

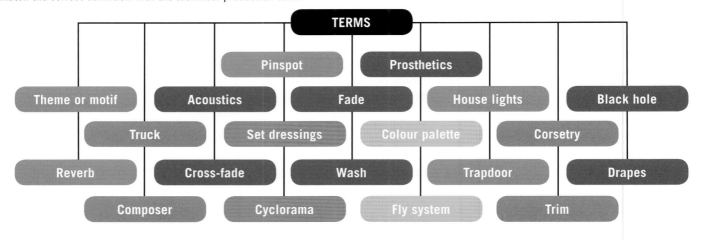

TERMS

- Pinspot
- Prosthetics
- Theme or motif
- Acoustics
- Fade
- House lights
- Black hole
- Truck
- Set dressings
- Colour palette
- Corsetry
- Reverb
- Cross-fade
- Wash
- Trapdoor
- Drapes
- Composer
- Cyclorama
- Fly system
- Trim

DEFINITIONS

1 A spotlight so tightly focused that it lights only a very small area, such as a single object or an actor's face.

2 Curtains or other hanging fabric.

3 A distinctive recurring section of music, often associated with a particular character or mood.

4 The range of colours used.

5 Additional pieces of make-up that can be attached, such as false noses, artificial wounds or horns.

6 A large semi-circular stretched curtain or screen, usually positioned upstage.

7 The sound quality in a given space, such as whether or not a theatrical space affects sound making it clear, echoing, warm or muffled and so on.

8 A means of raising and lowering scenery or other items onto the stage using a system of ropes and pulleys.

9 The lights in the auditorium that are usually up when the audience arrives and before the play begins.

10 Undergarments such as corsets, girdles and bustles used to shape a body and alter its silhouette.

11 Someone who writes music.

12 A lighting transition involving changing lighting states by bringing up the new state while reducing the old state.

13 A platform on wheels upon which scenery can be mounted and moved.

14 An area of the stage which has accidentally been left unlit.

15 Items on the set not actually used as props, but that create detail and interest, such as vases or framed paintings.

16 Additional decorative items such as fur on a collar or cuffs or a fringe on a jacket, dress or skirt.

17 An echoing effect, sustaining the sound longer than usual.

18 Gradually turning sound or lighting up or down.

19 Lighting that covers the entire stage.

20 A door in the floor of a stage allowing objects or performers to be dropped, lifted or lowered.

LEARNING CHECKLIST: SECTION C

Tick each aspect of 'Live theatre production' if you are confident of your knowledge and ability.

If you are unsure of anything, go back and revise.

Do you know...?

The specialisms you could choose to write about

The genre, style and period of the play you have seen and how they might affect the acting and design choices

How to make detailed notes about the production you have seen

How to select key moments or sections to write about

How to describe, analyse and evaluate

The technical terminology appropriate for different specialisms

Which characters you might choose to discuss if writing about performance

How to plan an answer to a question asking about a production you have seen

How to evaluate if the acting or designs are effective

Which examples you could discuss to demonstrate your knowledge of design skills

How to describe the impact of the acting or design choices on the audience

How to read the question

The questions in the Drama exam will vary from year to year, but it is always important when you are faced with the exam paper, that you *carefully* read the questions in front of you. In the heat of the moment, it is easy to misread a question. Some students make the mistake of answering a similar question that they have practised for rather than the one which is actually asked.

In order to make sure that you can fully answer a question, you might find the following approach useful.

▸ Underline key words.

▸ Double-check any references to a character or particular scenes to ensure that you will write about the correct ones.

▸ Pay attention to any bullet points. They are there to help you break down and fully grasp the question.

▸ Make notes around the question if you think straight away of some points you could make.

▸ As you read the extract given for Section B questions, underline or circle moments that you want to discuss, such as important lines or significant stage directions.

The following pages have example questions with typical points to look out for.

Section B: Study of a set play: *Blood Brothers*

1 You are designing a costume ① for Linda ② to wear in a performance of this extract. ③ The costume must reflect the context of *Blood Brothers* set in a Liverpool community in the 1970s. ④ Describe your design ideas for the costume. [4 marks]

① In this case, you are being asked to design a costume, but the question could be about other design skills, such as set, lighting or sound.

② Although there are two characters in the extract, you must write about Linda in this instance.

③ The characters age and change in *Blood Brothers*, so make sure your design ideas are appropriate for the specified extract.

④ The context is given as 1970s Liverpool. Other context questions might emphasise the 'working-class community' or when the characters are younger or the 1960s.

 TIP

This question requires a wide range of skills from you, including design and understanding of character, plot and context. It is tempting to spend too long on it, but as it worth relatively few marks, make sure you answer concisely.

2 You are performing the role of Mr Lyons. ①

Describe how you would use your vocal ② and physical ③ skills to perform the line below and explain the effects ④ you want to create:

Jennifer! Jennifer, how many times… the factory is here, my work is here… (page 44) [8 marks]

① Make sure you are writing about the correct character. It is useful to include a sentence about the character and their importance in the play or their emotional state before this line is spoken.

② Remember that appropriate vocal skills might include volume, accent, pace and emotional range, for example.

③ Physical skills might be gesture, movement, posture, gait, facial expressions.

④ What do you want to achieve? To show that Mr Lyons is angry? Frustrated? That he is in charge? What effect should he have on Mrs Lyons? What does his delivery of the line tell the audience about him?

 TIP

Although worth more marks than Question 1, you must also watch your timing on this question. You might want to aim for two or three vocal skills and two or three physical skills, but avoid over-writing. Remember to both **describe** what you would do and **explain** the effects you hope to achieve.

3 Focus on the shaded part of the extract (page 45, from 'Look, Jen' to 'I really do think you should see a doctor'). ①

You are performing the role of Mr Lyons. ②

Explain how you and the actor playing Mrs Lyons ③ might use the performance space ④ and interact ⑤ with each other to show the audience the tense relationship ⑥ between the characters. [12 marks]

① In the exam paper, the area to focus on will be shaded in grey and is included as part of a longer extract.

② Again, make sure you are writing about the correct character.

③ You could make reference to the other character and their actions in relation to your character.

④ Where are you positioned on the stage? When and where might you move? Will you use levels? Will your proximity to each other change?

⑤ How do you respond to each other? Do you react at a particular moment? Is there any physical contact or change in facial expressions?

⑥ In this instance, you are being asked to look at how a tense relationship is created. In another exam paper, you might be looking at creating a particular mood, style or emotion, such as romance or conflict.

TIP

When writing responses to acting questions like this, it is a good idea to write in the first person, so 'As Mr Lyons, I am frustrated by Mrs Lyons' worrying, but I will hide this when I try to calm her down by…'

4 You are performing the role of Mrs Lyons. ①

Describe how you would use your acting skills ② to portray Mrs Lyons' character.

Explain why your ideas ③ are appropriate for:

- This extract ④
- The performance of your role in the play as a whole. ⑤ [20 marks]

① Typically, Question 4 will focus on a different character in the extract from the one that was the focus for Question 3.

② Acting skills, unless otherwise specified, should include vocal and physical skills.

③ Consider your understanding of the character, their motivations and role in the play and how these ideas can be practically realised in performance.

④ You might want to focus on particular lines or stage directions from the extract in order to provide precise details.

⑤ You could choose two or three moments from other sections of the play and describe and analyse acting choices that could be made. Does the character change and develop, or are they consistent throughout?

TIP

Remember to use the correct acting terminology when writing about your acting choices. This is a good opportunity to demonstrate how your acting skills can convey the character's mental state, social status, development and importance to the play as a whole.

5 You are a designer working on **one** aspect of **design** ① for this extract. **Describe** ② how you would use your design skills to **create effects** ③ which **support the action** of this extract. ④ Explain why your ideas are appropriate for this extract and the play as a whole. ⑤ [20 marks]

 TIP

Remember that you will answer *either* Question 4 or Question 5.

① Note that you are to choose one design specialism to write about: lighting, costume, set or sound.

② Describe in detail, with terminology, your ideas for the extract.

③ What impact will your design choices have, for example creating a certain mood or location or enhancing an aspect of a character?

④ Specify how your design is appropriate for the particular scene given.

⑤ Provide practical examples of how your ideas can work in the rest of the play.

 TIP

Question 4 or Question 5 is worth the most marks in Section B, so make sure you allow the most time to answer it.

Section C: Understanding drama: Live theatre production

Performance

Describe ① how an actor used their acting skills ② to create an effective character ③ within the production. Analyse ④ and evaluate ⑤ how successful they were in communicating their role to the audience. ⑥

You could make reference to:

- Vocal skills, such as tone, accent, pace, pitch and emotional range ⑦
- Physical skills, such as gestures and movement ⑧
- A scene or key moments from the whole play. ⑨ [32 marks]

① Be clear when describing the performance because it is unlikely the examiner will have seen the same performance. You might be asked to describe a single character or you might have the option to write about several.

② Unless otherwise specified, this should include vocal and physical skills.

③ Another exam paper might ask something different, such as, how the role was conveyed to an audience or how convincing a performance was.

④ Break down the specifics of the performance.

⑤ Did the performance work? If so, why? If not, why not?

⑥ What impact did the performance have on the audience?

⑦ Bullet points provide helpful prompts, but don't be restricted by them if you want to discuss other vocal skills, for example.

⑧ Depending on the performance, you could discuss other physical skills.

⑨ You might be prompted to look at a scene or section, key moments or the play as a whole. It is a good idea to prepare in advance several sections or moments you could write about, then make your final choices based on the question before you.

Design

Ray Fearon and Tara Fitzgerald in Macbeth *at the Globe* ▲

Describe how costumes ① were used to support the style ② of the production. Analyse and evaluate how successful ③ the costumes were in helping to convey the style to the audience. ④

You could make reference to:

- The fabrics and other materials used ⑤
- The colour and textures used ⑥
- Hair, make-up and accessories ⑦
- A scene or the production as a whole. ⑧ [32 marks]

① The design specialism is identified as costume in this section and the plural word 'costumes' indicates, in this case, that you should describe more than one, if possible.

② The style of the production could involve a discussion on whether the costumes are realistic and naturalistic, symbolic, comic or representative of a particular period. Other papers might ask you to focus on whether the costumes help to convey characterisation and/or the action and plot of the play.

③ You must remember to evaluate the costumes, judging if they worked well and if so, why, and if not, why not.

④ This invites you to discuss the impact on the audience, for example, the first impression a costume created or if a costume showed a character or situation developing or changing.

⑤ This bullet point is a helpful prompt, but, depending on the production you have seen, you might have additional points you wish to make.

⑥ Remember to use correct costume terminology throughout. Although this prompt asks about colour, simply writing that a character 'wears a red dress' won't gain you many marks. Look for more details and technical features.

⑦ Precise details about these could boost your marks.

⑧ In this case, you are being given the choice of a scene — the length of which you may choose yourself — or the whole play. If you write about the whole play, choose a few key costumes rather than spreading yourself too thinly.

 TIP

Typically, Section C will have one acting question and two questions on named design specialisms. You cannot assume that any specific question will be asked. You might only prepare, say, a lighting question, but find when you open the paper that lighting is not one of the specialisms named.

 TIP

Section C has the single question worth the most marks, so make sure you allow enough time for it.

Making plans

You will need to be aware of timing in the exam, and you will probably find that you have relatively little time for planning. It is certainly worth, however, taking a couple of minutes to plan for some of the questions worth the most marks, such as Section B Questions 4 or 5 or your choice of question in Section C.

The following are a few brief suggestions of how to make a plan.

Annotating the question

You could note some key words around the question as you read it, for example:

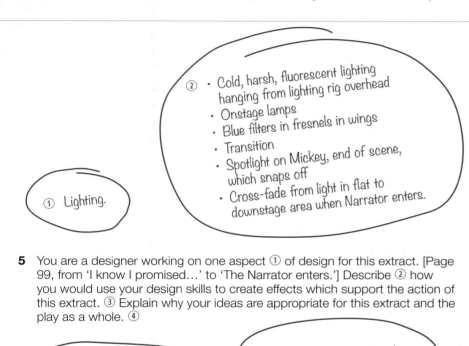

① Lighting.

② • Cold, harsh, fluorescent lighting hanging from lighting rig overhead
• Onstage lamps
• Blue filters in fresnels in wings
• Transition
• Spotlight on Mickey, end of scene, which snaps off
• Cross-fade from light in flat to downstage area when Narrator enters.

5 You are a designer working on one aspect ① of design for this extract. [Page 99, from 'I know I promised…' to 'The Narrator enters.'] Describe ② how you would use your design skills to create effects which support the action of this extract. ③ Explain why your ideas are appropriate for this extract and the play as a whole. ④

③ Effects:
• Shows distance between Mickey and Linda
• Mickey walks into darkness
• Contrast with Narrator.

④ Ideas for the rest of the play:
• Combination of naturalistic and stylised lighting
• Contrast with lighting used for the robbery and the end of the play:
– colour filters
– followspots
– transitions
– flashing lights.

A mind map

Another flexible and quick way of drawing up a plan is to create a mind map. For example:

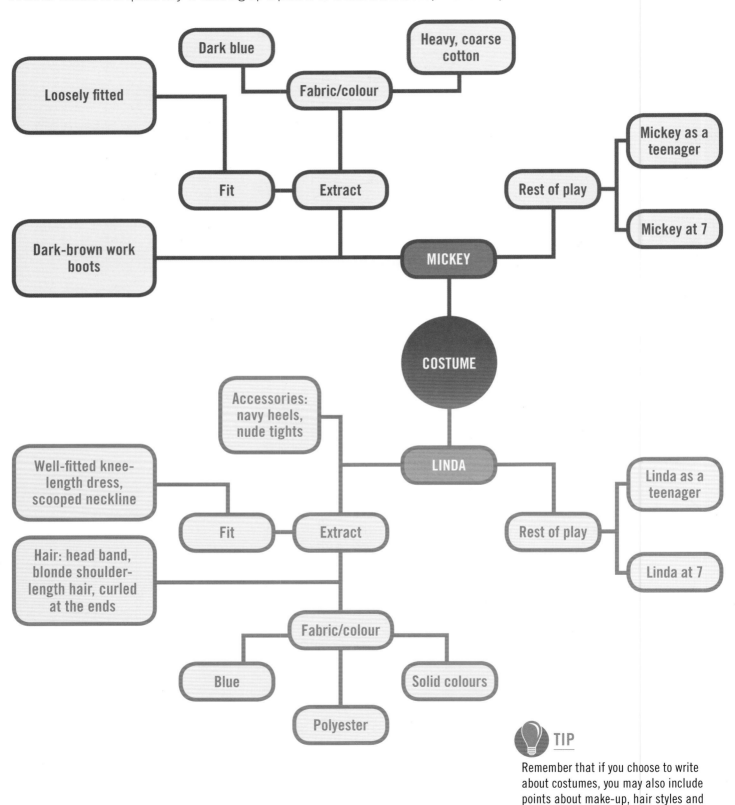

TIP

Remember that if you choose to write about costumes, you may also include points about make-up, hair styles and accessories.

Lists

After you have read through a question, you could quickly make a list of points you want to make and then go back and tick off the items once you have included them in your answer.

<u>Acting Mickey</u>

<u>This extract:</u>

<u>Physical:</u>

- Gait/stance: Defeated, shuffling, effects of addiction.
- Gestures: Reaches out for pills.
- Pace: Slow, hesitant.
- Eye contact: Avoids Linda's gaze.

<u>Vocal:</u>

- Volume: Softly spoken, until speech about 'You and Councillor Eddie Lyons'.
- Accent: Liverpool working-class accent.
- Emotional range: Little emotion shown, until bitterness about Eddie comes out.

<u>Rest of play:</u>

- Mickey at 7: High energy, uses levels, comic.
- Mickey at 14: Self-conscious, comic.
- Effects created: Sympathy for Mickey.
- Action of play: Mickey seen as victim of circumstances/ injustice – from lively, funny boy to defeated, desperate man.

 TIP

Remember that, if it helps you, you can draw a quick sketch to clarify your design ideas as part of your answer. For example, Mickey in the pill scene:

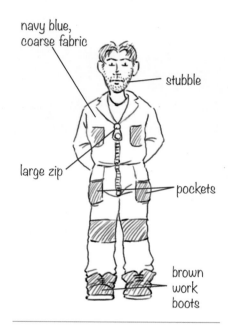

 **LOOK HERE**

See pages 67, 68 and 76 for other examples of planning an exam response.

Shaping and improving the quality of your writing

Well-organised and clearly developed writing makes a positive impression and will help you to avoid common exam mistakes, such as drifting off topic or repeating yourself.

Some ideas for improving your answers include:

- ▸ Use some of the wording from the question. For example, if the question asks you to use your skills to 'create tension', make sure that the phrase appears at least once (and probably more frequently) in your response.
- ▸ Think about the order in which you write about your ideas. You might quickly number any ideas in any plans you have made in order to confirm the order.
- ▸ Check over your work to make sure you have answered each aspect of the question. You might use your plan or the bullet points provided in some questions and tick these off once you have written about them.

 TIP

Avoid over-writing on questions only worth a few marks. If there are only 4 marks available for a question, no matter how much or how brilliantly you write, you will not be awarded more than that.

Using discursive markers

Discursive markers are phrases that you can use to link, order or otherwise clarify your ideas. Think of them as signposts which help the reader to understand in what order you want them to consider your ideas or which ideas are to be contrasted or highlighted. Use of discursive markers can give you writing a better flow and make it easier to understand, as well as helping you to express more sophisticated ideas.

Some examples of discursive markers include:

Ordering
first, second, to begin, initially, next, finally, ultimately, in conclusion

Emphasising
most importantly, significantly, remarkably

Comparing and contrasting
similarly, in contrast, both, in the same way, rather than

Providing examples
for instance, for example, in this case

Building an argument
additionally, in addition, another

Providing contrasting points of view
however, but, in spite of this

Task 1

Read this excerpt from a student-style answer and underline each example of a discursive marker.

> Initially, the sound designer used a range of recorded and live sound effects in order to create a sense of menace. An example of this was the contrasting use of recorded classical music with the sudden offstage sound of breaking glass. In addition, she experimented with the location of the sounds, some seeming to come from behind or to the sides of the audience, while others clearly originated from the stage. However, the effect was not always successful because of the low volume used.

Task 2

Write a paragraph about a production you have seen. In it, introduce at least three discursive markers to clarify your ideas.

Checking your work for typical errors

Every year, there are some common errors made in the exam, costing students marks. Below are some examples and possible solutions.

Running out of time

The exam lasts 1 hour and 45 minutes and is worth 80 marks in total. You need to allow time for reading the questions and extract, planning your response and checking your work, so that means you have only a little more than a minute per mark of writing time. Therefore, you need to use your time wisely. Here are some suggestions for good time-keeping:

▸ Practise working on a real examination question paper, making sure you can quickly locate the questions you need to answer.

▸ Practise writing to a time limit. Some students find it helpful early in the course to write untimed responses so that they can thoroughly explore their ideas, but gradually introduce writing to a fixed time, so, by the time they come to the exam, they are very used to the correct timings.

▸ Think about the order in which you complete the questions. You can answer them in any order. Some students prefer to undertake the examination in the order that the questions are asked, using the low-mark questions as a warm up and confidence-builder before answering the questions that are worth more marks. Alternatively, you might start with the questions worth the most marks. Some students choose to answer the questions in reverse, starting with Section C and finishing with Section A.

▸ Make sure, however, that you answer every question. If you leave out, for example, Section C or a valuable question from Section B, it will cost you dearly.

 TIP

As you prepare and practise in the build up to the exam, it is worth experimenting with different timings. Make sure that you are able to answer all of the questions fully in the time allowed.

 TIP

This is not an exam where you should expect to have any time left over at the end. There is no advantage to completing your work early.

▸ Make a plan for how long you will spend on each section. There is no set way of doing this, but here is an example of one candidate's plan that you might find useful:

- – Section A: 5 minutes
- – Section B: 50 minutes
- – Section C: 40 minutes
- – Reading/checking: 10 minutes.

Writing that is too general

Although you might have very strong ideas of what you want to achieve through your use of acting or design, you must make sure that you present these ideas in a precise and clear way.

Task 3

Read the candidate-style response below about the lighting at the beginning of *Blood Brothers*. After reading the annotation questions to prompt improvement, rewrite the paragraph with more precise details.

> I would have the stage very dark at the beginning of the play. ① The Narrator would step into a spotlight. ② When Mrs Johnstone comes on, she would be in a different pool of light. ③ I want the mood to be different when the Milkman comes on, so will have a lighter wash of lighting at this point. ④

① What will the lighting state be here? A blackout? A fade up?

② What colour will the spotlight be? What angle will it be? How bright?

③ Where will this light be in relation to the light on the Narrator? Downstage? Upstage? What colour filter will you use? What angle will the lantern be?

④ How will you handle this transition? Will you use a cross-fade? What colour will this wash of light be? What lanterns will you use to create it?

Omitting technical terms

Technical vocabulary is important in showing that you understand the different aspects, skills and techniques of live theatre. Failing to use them in an exam response might suggest that there are gaps in your learning or understanding.

TIP

Remember that the Section C question will not provide the name of the production you saw, so don't waste time looking for it. Also remember that your Section C play cannot be the same as your Section B set text.

TIP

Try to locate particular moments or particular lines of dialogue when effects might occur.

Task 4

Read the following two example responses about the performance of Mrs Lyons on page 22. Highlight the technical terminology used.

Which do you think is the more effective answer?

My aim is to show the two sides of Mrs Lyons: a proper middle-class woman and a desperate, unhappy woman who will do anything to get what she wants. As Mrs Lyons I would use Received Pronunciation, with a voice which is low and well-modulated when I am confident, but rises in pitch and volume when I am stressed, such as when I say the word 'Mine'. Although I try to give the appearance of being in control by having an upright posture and holding my head high, my gestures frequently give away what I am really thinking. For example, when I suggest that it is time Mrs Johnstone, left, I wring my hands nervously, showing I am afraid of this confrontation. Realising that I might appear weak, I cross my arms defensively while saying in a loud, demanding voice, 'we're not satisfied', emphasising 'we're'. A strong physical choice I make is to 'drag' Mrs Johnstone away from the cot. I will lunge at Mrs Johnstone and pull her hard by the arm, keeping in very close proximity to her. My expression will show my lack of control: my eyes large, my mouth in an angry grimace. We will be off-balance and almost tumble over, showing how out of control I am.

Mrs Lyons wants to get rid of Mrs Johnstone, so she stands over her and speaks in a posh voice. She speaks quite loudly because she wants her to go. She points to the door on the word 'left' and stares at Mrs Johnstone for a long time. Some of the scene might go quite quickly but other bits might be slow. The two women should practically get into a fistfight at one point which would be very dramatic. I want the audience to see that Mrs Lyons is a bit out of her mind and they shouldn't like her at all.

 TIP

It might seem obvious, but make sure that in Section B you answer about the set text you have studied in Drama. Every year, there are students who write about another play, such as one they have studied in English. The demands of English and Drama are different, and, for the Drama exam, you will need to write about the play you have studied on your Drama course.

Task 5

Write a paragraph about the same scene as in Task 4, but instead discuss how you would perform Mrs Johnstone. Use technical terminology whenever you can.

Sample question paper

For practice, you might like to attempt this exam paper under timed exam conditions.

Section A: Theatre roles and terminology

1 In the professional theatre, who is responsible for operating the technical equipment such as the sound board?

   A The sound designer.

   B The stage manager.

   C The technician.   [1 mark]

2 When performing in a promenade production, which of the following do you need to consider?

   A How you will use the proscenium and apron area of the stage.

   B The health and safety of the audience as they follow the actors around the set.

   C Where to store large set items in the theatre's wings.   [1 mark]

3 What type of stage is shown in Figure 1?

   A A traverse stage.

   B An end on stage.

   C A thrust stage.   [1 mark]

4 In Figure 1, where is the actor standing?

   A Upstage right.

   B Downstage right.

   C Downstage left.   [1 mark]

Figure 1

Section B: Study of a Set Play: *Blood Brothers*

Focus on an extract on pages 83–84, from 'Throughout the following' to 'Edward: Can I write to you?'

5.1 You are designing the lighting for a performance of this extract. The setting must reflect the context of *Blood Brothers*, set in a working-class community in the 1970s. Describe your design ideas for the setting.   [4 marks]

5.2 You are performing the role of Edward.

Describe how you would use your vocal and physical skills to perform the line below and explain the effects you want to create:

'I go away to university tomorrow.'   [8 marks]

5.3 You are performing the role of Edward.

Focus on 'Well, hello, sweetie pie' to 'Can I write to you?'

Explain how you and the actor playing Linda might use the performance space and interact with each other to establish the emotional relationship between them for the audience.   [12 marks]

And EITHER

5.4 You are performing the role of Linda.

Describe how you would use your acting skills to interpret Linda's character in this extract, and explain why your ideas are appropriate both for this extract and the play as a whole. [20 marks]

OR

5.5 You are a designer working on one aspect of design for this extract.

Describe how you would use your design skills to create effects which support the action of this extract, and explain why your ideas are appropriate both for this extract and the play as a whole. [20 marks]

Section C: Live theatre production

Answer **one** question from this section.

State the title of the live theatre production you saw:

11 Describe how one actor in the play you saw used their acting skills to create an appropriate and interesting character. Analyse and evaluate how successful they were in communicating their character to the audience.

You should make reference to:

- The actor's use of the performance space
- The actor's use of vocal and physical skills
- The actor's understanding of the character's motivations and background. [32 marks]

OR

12 Describe how sound was used to support the style and context of the production. Analyse and evaluate how successfully the sound design was in communicating the meaning and mood of the production to the audience.

You could make reference to:

- Types of sound/music
- Use of specific sound effects
- How the sound was created and amplified. [32 marks]

OR

13 Describe how costumes were used to enhance the characterisations of one or more characters in the play. Analyse and evaluate how successful the costumes were in helping to communicate the character's or characters' importance in the action of the play and any changes or development they undergo.

You could make reference to:

- The materials used
- The shape/fit/silhouette
- The colour/texture. [32 marks]

 TIP

Section B in the exam consists of Questions 5 to 10, including questions about the other set texts. You will need to locate the set of questions relevant to *Blood Brothers*.

LEARNING CHECKLIST: EXAMINATION PRACTICE

Tick each aspect of exam preparation if you are confident of your knowledge.

If you are unsure of anything, read through this section again.

Do you know...?

How to look for key words in the questions

The difference between your Section B and Section C texts

How to avoid running out of time

How to include detail and refer to specific examples

How to plan an answer

How to use discursive markers

How to include technical terminology

The range of questions you could be asked

Answers to 'Test yourself' questions

Test yourself 1 (page 5)

1 Section C.
2 4.
3 Section B.
4 40 per cent.
5 Section A.
6 The glossary.

Test yourself A2 (page 12)

1 Traverse.
2 Promenade.
3 End on.

Test yourself A3 (page 19)

A Thrust.
B End on.
C Traverse.
D Theatre in the round.
E Promenade.
F Proscenium arch.

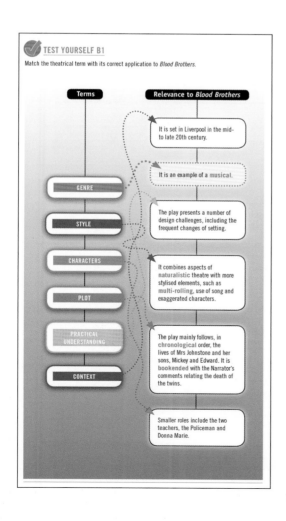

Test yourself A1 (page 9) ▼

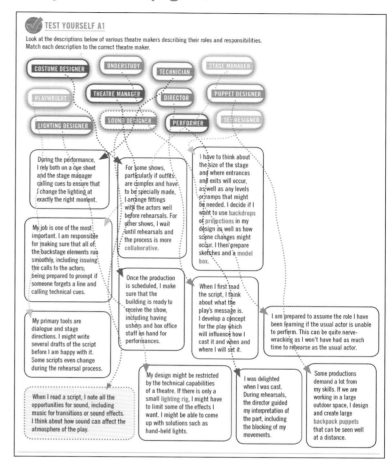

◄ **Test yourself B1 (page 23)**

Test yourself B2 (page 26)

1 Act 2.
2 Seven years.
3 Mrs Lyons says that she can provide better for him.
4 Mrs Lyons.
5 Act 1.

Test yourself B3 (page 27) ▸

Test yourself B4 (page 31)

1 The Johnstones.

2 Mickey (and the Dole-ites).

3 Mickey and Linda.

4 Edward.

5 Edward.

6 Mr Lyons.

7 Mr Lyons.

8 A better education, leading to a good job.

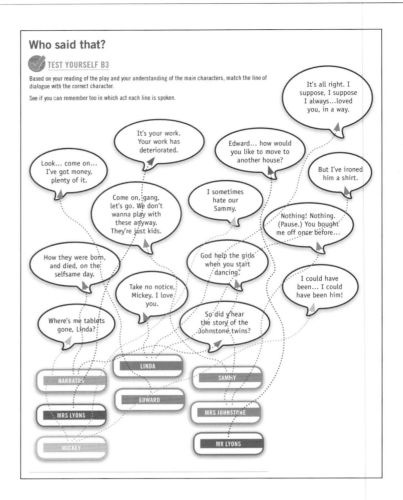

Test yourself B5 (page 43) ▾

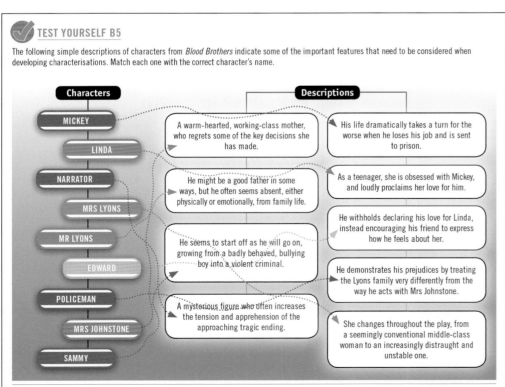

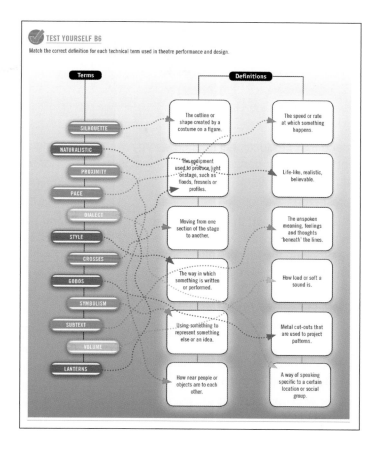

TEST YOURSELF B6

Match the correct definition for each technical term used in theatre performance and design.

Terms

SILHOUETTE
NATURALISTIC
PROXIMITY
PACE
DIALECT
STYLE
CROSSES
GOBOS
SYMBOLISM
SUBTEXT
VOLUME
LANTERNS

Definitions

The outline or shape created by a costume on a figure.

The speed or rate at which something happens.

The equipment used to produce light onstage, such as floods, fresnels or profiles.

Life-like, realistic, believable.

Moving from one section of the stage to another.

The unspoken meaning, feelings and thoughts 'beneath' the lines.

The way in which something is written or performed.

How loud or soft a sound is.

Using something to represent something else or an idea.

Metal cut-outs that are used to project patterns.

How near people or objects are to each other.

A way of speaking specific to a certain location or social group.

Test yourself B6 (page 80) ▶

Test yourself C1 (page 83)

1 Costume.
2 Set.
3 Sound.
4 Set.
5 Performance.
6 Lighting.
7 Sound.
8 Costume.

Test yourself C2 (page 121)

1 Set.
2 Performance.
3 Sound.
4 Costume.
5 Performance.
6 Lighting.
7 Set.
8 Sound.
9 Sound.
10 Costume.
11 Lighting.
12 Sound.

Test yourself C3 (page 122)

1 Pinspot.
2 Drapes.
3 Theme or motif.
4 Colour palette.
5 Prosthetics.
6 Cyclorama.
7 Acoustics.
8 Fly system.
9 House lights.
10 Corsetry.
11 Composer.
12 Cross-fade.
13 Truck.
14 Black hole.
15 Set dressings.
16 Trim.
17 Reverb.
18 Fade.
19 Wash.
20 Trapdoor.

GLOSSARY

Adrenaline: A hormone that produces heightened energy and excitement when facing dangerous, frightening or competitive situations.

Affluent: Wealthy, prosperous, well off.

Alienation effect: A distancing effect that prevents the audience from believing they are watching a real event. It might involve breaking the fourth wall by speaking directly to the audience or drawing attention to the mechanics behind the play's production.

Amplification: How sounds are made louder, usually through the use of microphones or other sound-boosting equipment.

Analyse: To examine something, perhaps by looking at the different elements of it, and to explain it.

Antagonist: A character who opposes, works against or brings down the protagonist.

Apron: The front area of the stage, nearest the audience, which projects in front of the curtain.

Audience interaction: Directly involving members of the audience in the play, for example, by bringing them onstage, going into the audience to speak with them, asking for a response from onstage, or passing them props to hold.

Backpack puppets: Large puppets attached to the puppeteer by a backpack-like device.

Backdrop: A large painted cloth that serves as scenery, often at the back of the stage.

Barn doors: Metal flaps used on fresnel lanterns to shape the light beam into a particular shape, such as a square. They also lessen the 'spill' of light, ensuring that exactly the correct area is lit.

Block: Set the movements made by the actors.

Bookended: A structural device in which a story ends at a similar point to where it began.

Box set: A set with three complete walls, often used in naturalistic set designs, for example to create a believable room.

Call the cues: Announce instructions, for example, telling technicians when lighting or sound changes should occur.

Chairography: Choreographed movement involving moving or rearranging chairs on the stage.

Characters: The people involved in the action of a play, film or novel.

Choral character: A character who comments on the action of a play, while also participating in some of the action.

Chronological: Events presented in the order in which they occurred.

Climax: The moment of highest tension in a play, usually of great importance, and often the culmination of earlier events.

Collaborative: A process where people work together rather than individually.

Colour palette: The range of colours used. For example, a scene might use light colours, dark colours, muted tones, grey tones, earth tones or vivid, primary colours.

Comic relief: Light-hearted or humorous characters or interludes that provide a break from more intense, serious sections of a drama.

Composite set: A single set that represents several locations at once.

Concept: A unifying idea about the production, such as how it will be interpreted and performed.

Crosses: Movements from one section of the stage to another.

Counter-crosses: Movement in opposition to another character's cross, so, one going stage left when the other goes stage right. This might be to balance the stage picture or to demonstrate an aspect of the characters' relationship.

Covering (a role): Learning the words and movements for a part that you do not usually perform.

Describe: To give details of what you saw, heard or experienced.

Dialect: A way of speaking that is specific to a certain location or social group.

Domestic: Related to activities in a home or within a family.

Dramatic irony: When the audience knows something that one or more characters on stage do not.

End on: A staging configuration in which the audience sits along one end of the stage (the front), directly facing it.

Ensemble: A group of actors. In some productions, ensemble members might play additional small roles and/or act as a chorus.

Entourage: A group of people who escort or assist an important person.

Epic: A type of early 20th-century theatre particularly associated with Bertolt Brecht. It is non-naturalistic theatre that uses particular techniques to remind the audience they are watching a play.

Expressionistic: A non-naturalistic style that highlights subjective emotions.

Evaluate: To judge or form an opinion, such as explaining what effect was created and how successful it was.

Flats: Pieces of scenery mounted on frames, for example, representing walls.

Fly space: The area above the stage where scenery might be stored and lowered to the stage.

Followspot: A powerful spotlight operated so that its beam follows an actor around the stage.

Fourth wall: An imaginary wall that separates the actors from the audience, giving the impression that the world of the actors is entirely distinct from that of the audience.

Fresnel: A lantern with a lens that produces a soft-edged beam of light.

Front of house: Ushers and other members of theatre staff who deal with the audience, as opposed to those who work backstage.

Genre: A category or type of music, art or literature, usually with its own typical conventions.

Gobo: A metal cut-out used to project patterns, such as leaves, stars, swirls or waves.

Immersive: A type of theatre where the audience are in the middle of the action of the performance, without the sense of separation usually associated with going to the theatre. They might be required to wear masks, costumes or to follow certain characters.

Interpretation: Bringing out a particular meaning by making specific choices. In this case, choices about how a play could be performed and designed in order to get across a particular meaning. There might be many different interpretations possible.

Intonation: The rise and fall of pitch in the voice; the musicality of speech.

Lighting plot: A guide to the lighting of a production, including the location and types of various lighting instruments and a scene-by-scene list of lighting requirements.

Lighting rig: The structure that holds the lighting equipment in the theatre (usually in the roof).

Lighting states: The settings and positions of lighting to create certain lighting conditions, such as a bright afternoon or a moonlit scene.

Love interest: A character whose primary importance is their romantic relationship with a central character.

Minimalist: Simple, spare; using few elements; stripped back.

Model box: A three-dimensional scale-model of the set that shows how the real set will look and work.

Monotone: A voice that doesn't change in pitch, pace or expression.

Motivations: The feelings behind what a character wants or needs, in a particular scene.

Multi-rolling: When one actor plays more than one character (multiple roles).

Musical: A type of play in which music, singing and dancing play a significant part.

Naturalistic: Lifelike, believable, realistic.

Nature versus nurture: An area of debate that seeks to determine if there are genetic and biological issues (nature) that determine a person's characteristics and behaviour or whether environmental issues, including home life and education (nurture) are more important.

Pace: The speed or rate at which something happens.

Pitch: How high or low a voice is.

Phrasing: How the words in a line of speech are grouped together. For example, whether a line is said on a single breath or broken into fragments.

Plot: The sequence of main events of a play, film or novel.

Practical: Something that can actually be physically done, rather than simply an idea.

Pristine: As if new; perfect; clean.

Projections: A technique where moving or still images are projected to form a theatrical backdrop.

Prompt book: A copy of the production script of the play, which includes detailed information about the play's blocking, props and other technical elements.

Props: Small items that actors can carry, such as books, a hairbrush, a package or a mug.

Protagonist: The leading character in a play.

Proximity: How near people or objects are to each other; also referred to as 'proxemics', which describes the relative positions of characters on stage.

Received pronunciation (RP): A way of speaking which is considered the 'standard' form of English pronunciation. It is not specific to a certain location, but, instead, is associated with education and formal speaking.

Register: The vocal range of the voice (upper, middle or lower register) and the variety of tones of voice.

Set dressings: Items on the set not actually used as props, but that create detail and interest in it, such as vases or framed paintings on a wall.

Sightlines: The view the audience has of the stage and/or dramatic action. If a sightline is blocked or restricted, for example by a poorly placed piece of furniture, it means that some audience members cannot see part of the stage.

Silhouette: The outline or shape created by a costume on a figure.

Sound plot: A list of the sound effects or music needed and any sound equipment that will be used. This is usually organised scene-by-scene and might contain information such as cues and volume.

Staging configuration: The type of stage and audience arrangement.

Stage picture: A term for a well-arranged visual stage image which conveys a certain impression to the audience. This is also called a 'tableau'.

Status: The social or professional standing of a character.

Still image: An acting technique when you freeze a moment in silence, showing the characters' physical positions and facial expressions.

Subliminally: In a way that barely registers: the audience is affected without consciously being aware of what is affecting them.

Strobe: A lighting device that produces short bursts of light.

Style: The way in which something is created or performed.

Stylised: Non-realistic, heightened, exaggerated; done in a particular manner that perhaps emphasises one element.

Subtext: The unspoken meaning, feelings and thoughts 'beneath' the lines, which might be shown in the characters' body language, tone of voice and facial expressions.

Symbolic: Using something to represent something else. For example, the Narrator might be a figure who symbolises the unemployed of Liverpool.

Tragicomic: A creative work, such as a play or novel, with both tragic and comic elements.

Truck: A platform on wheels upon which scenery can be mounted and moved.

Virtuoso: Highly skilled; expert in an artistic skill, such as music, dance or acting.

Volatile: Likely to change suddenly; explosive; unpredictable.

Wing space: An area to the side of the stage. This is the space where actors, unseen by the audience, wait to enter and where props and set pieces can be stored.